A. PHILIP RANDOLPH

MAKERS OF AMERICA

A. PHILIP RANDOLPH
MESSENGER FOR THE MASSES

LILLIE PATTERSON

☑®

Facts On File, Inc.

AN INFOBASE HOLDINGS COMPANY

A. Philip Randolph: Messenger for the Masses

Facts On File, Inc.
11 Penn Plaza
New York, NY 10001

Library of Congress Cataloging-in-Publication Data

Patterson, Lillie.
    A. Philip Randolph : messenger for the masses / Lillie Patterson
        p.   cm.— (Makers of America)
    Includes bibliographical references and index.
    ISBN 0-8160-2827-3 (alk. paper)
    1. Randolph, A. Philip (Asa Philip), 1889–1979—Juvenile
literature.   2. Afro-Americans—Biography—Juvenile literature.
3. Civil rights workers—United States—Biography—Juvenile
literature.   I. Title.   II. Series: Makers of America (Facts On File, Inc.)
E185.97.R27P38   1995
323'.092—dc20
[B]   95–17165

Facts On File books are available at special discounts when purchased in bulk quantities for businesses, associations, institutions or sales promotions. Please call our Special Sales Department in New York at 212/967-8800 or 800/322-8755.

Text design by Debbie Glasserman
Jacket design by Duane Stapp

VB FOF 10 9 8 7 6 5 4 3 2 1

This book is printed on acid-free paper.

Printed in the United States of America

For my brother and sisters
Alex, Mary and Anne Alexandria

CONTENTS

A. PHILIP RANDOLPH

1

THE MOWM
1940–1942

"Only power can affect the enforcement
and adoption of a given policy, and power
is the active principle of only the organized
masses, the masses organized for a
definite purpose."

—A. Philip Randolph

Standing six feet tall and elegantly erect, Asa Philip Randolph held the listening audience in rapt attention. His magnetic voice, fine-tuned for singing or speaking, challenged members of his race to show their loyalty and assert their rights as United States citizens. On that September night in 1940, Randolph issued a challenge to his race and to all citizens of his nation. He called upon black citizens to fight for jobs in national defense. He counseled listeners to insist upon the right of African Americans to fight alongside whites in the armed forces of the nation. He called upon them to march to put an end to all the Jim Crow practices that legalized segregation between blacks and whites, especially in all government departments and in defense jobs.

As president of the Brotherhood of Sleeping Car Porters, the organization of workers who serviced Pullman cars on trains, Randolph made this challenge to the audience of men and women who assembled as delegates from all sections of the United States.

By 1940, Randolph's reputation as a brilliant and tough labor organizer was well established. During the era when almost all trade unions refused membership to African Americans, and very few black unions existed, Randolph had waged and won a struggle to organize black railroad workers in the teeth of employer opposition, blacklisting and intimidation. Equally remarkable, Randolph had made strong labor alliances in 1936 and the Brotherhood of Sleeping Car Porters was accepted as a full international member of the American Federation of Labor.

When Randolph, who was generally known by his initials APR, spoke to a packed New York hall that night in September, 1940, he was 51 years of age, and at the pinnacle of his career as an American national labor organizer. He was now about to call for and lead a struggle of *all* black American workers for the right to apply for and to receive jobs and training in the nation's defense plants on the same basis as all other workers, free of the racial discrimination that until now had shut them out.

Randolph was set to devote his life to a struggle to end all forms of racial discrimination. He was poised to ask for the support of millions of white people in this effort.

As Randolph stood on that platform in 1940, he was about to enter a *second* career as an organizer and leader of the American civil rights movement itself, as a designer of the great alliance of the American popular front which would eventually uphold and nourish that movement in the mid-sixties.

Seated in the crowd and listening intently to Randolph's words was Eleanor Roosevelt, wife of the United States' president, Franklin Delano Roosevelt, and a scheduled speaker for the Brotherhood banquet the following evening. The First Lady had become a beloved friend of black citizens and had worked to help families secure jobs and food during the Great Depression that followed the stock market crash of 1929.

The First Lady had already advised her husband to give attention to racial segregation in the armed services after being alerted by Dr. Mary McLeod Bethune, who founded Cookman College in Daytona Beach, Florida, a school that later merged with Cookman Institute to become Bethune Cookman College. Dr. Bethune had come to Washington to head the new Office of Minority Affairs of the National Youth Administration. She shared with Eleanor Roosevelt a mutual interest in educating young people and helping them secure scholarship funds to earn college degrees.

Dr. Bethune had alerted her friend, Eleanor Roosevelt, of the mounting unrest over continued racial segregation in the military. Also, Thurgood Marshall, at that time the Chief Counsel for the Defense Fund of the NAACP (National Association for the Advancement of Colored People), had written to warn Henry L. Stimson, Secretary of War, that black troops would prefer to go to jail than continue to work amid the rigid racial segregation in the military.

Secretary Stimson shared Marshall's letter with Eleanor Roosevelt, who sent it to her husband along with a note to remind him of the need for a meeting with black leaders on the subject of how their race could participate in the armed services. She suggested that such a meeting be held soon.

It was. The meeting took place on September 27, 1940. Three leaders arrived for a conference with President Roosevelt. The tall figure of Randolph was easily recognized as he led the way. Accompanying him were Walter White, the well-known president of the NAACP, and T. Arnold Hill, an administrator with the Urban League.

Randolph reminded Roosevelt that the draft law did not abolish the discriminatory practices that separated fighting forces along racial identification in all of America's wars. Army and navy *officers* were white. The troops were kept in segregated units with all-black units assigned menial roles such as digging ditches, building roads, cooking and washing dishes and were therefore not promoted to positions as officers.

White and Hill mentioned other discriminatory rules practiced by industries, including those receiving lucrative government contracts. Black workers were still refused membership in trade unions and thus were not usually hired by large companies with the highest wage scales.

President Roosevelt listened intently, asking questions now and then. When the conference ended, he thanked the three leaders for coming and promised to get in touch with them within a few days. Randolph, Hill and White left on a high note of hope and anticipation. They waited for word from the president.

The response came not from Roosevelt but from Steve Early, Roosevelt's press secretary, who shared it with newspaper reporters at a press conference. Early reminded the newsmen of the president's conference with black leaders, then distributed printed copies of a statement drafted by the War

Department, a statement of policy regarding Negroes in national defense.

Randolph later read the wording of the press copy which stated that the policy of the War Department was not to intermingle colored and white enlisted personnel in the same regimental organizations. Worse, the press secretary alluded to "the plan on which we all agreed," implying that Randolph, Hill and White had sanctioned the plan.

Fury spurred Randolph to immediate action. Over the next few days, he joined White and Hill in publicizing the true intent of their conference with Roosevelt. Meanwhile, the three men tried to schedule another meeting with the president. None was granted. Steve Early refused to issue a clarification of his statement to the press.

Outraged, Randolph pondered how he might force the president and all Americans to bring about changes to end racist customs and rules. He sat brooding over this problem as he rode a train on his way to conduct conferences with Pullman porters in several states. Traveling with him was Milton Webster, the fearless, heavy-set former Pullman porter who had been fired for daring to organize Chicago porters into a local Brotherhood. Undaunted, Webster assisted Randolph in developing Brotherhood unions in many major American cities. The two men often traveled together to assist and motivate the Brotherhood members.

On that day in 1940, as the train sped through the lovely Virginia landscape, Randolph sat silent for a time, then suddenly turned to Webster. "We are going to have to do something about it." Webster sensed that his boss and friend was about to share a bold plan.

Randolph's idea was indeed revolutionary. He suggested that 10,000 Negroes could march on Washington in protest. Webster nodded agreement. He knew that whenever Randolph had conceived a plan, bold action would soon follow.

It was in Savannah, Georgia's oldest city, that Randolph proposed to Pullman porters the vision of a March on Washington to protest continued racial discrimination. The idea thrilled some listeners; it frightened others. At Brotherhood meetings in city after city most porters were ready for black Americans to confront the slave-master relationships that had stilted racial harmony and understanding for centuries. Polite pleading and protests had not brought about change. It was time to adopt Randolph's more assertive slogan: "We loyal Negro Americans demand the right to work and fight for our country."

In this mood, Randolph and other bold leaders issued a ringing challenge to Americans to join in the March on Washington for Jobs and Equal Participation in National Defense scheduled for July 1, 1941. The days of fruitless pleading had passed, Randolph insisted. Power must flow from the masses. Such a march, he hoped, would force President Roosevelt and other politicians to pass new civil rights laws.

Leaders of religious and civic organizations joined Randolph in planning the ambitious project. The March was designed to include a rally at the Lincoln Memorial. Eleanor Roosevelt would be invited as one of the speakers.

So the call went out. Newspapers, especially those owned by African-American publishers, kept readers informed. Churches and social groups inspired members to raise funds and make plans for the trip to Washington. The NAACP and the Urban League, along with other organized groups, publicized the project and coordinated efforts.

"Let the Negro masses speak!" Randolph repeated to audiences gathered at crowded conventions or standing on ghetto street corners.

In January 1941, he issued his call for a march scheduled for July 1, 1941:

> Dear fellow Negro Americans, be not dismayed in these terrible times. You possess power, great power. Our problem is to hitch it up for action on the broadest, daring, and most gigantic scale.
>
> In this period of power politics, nothing counts but pressure, and still more pressure, through the tactic and strategy of broad, organized, aggressive mass action behind the vital and important issues of the Negro. To this end, we propose that ten thousand Negroes MARCH ON WASHINGTON FOR JOBS IN NATIONAL DEFENSE AND EQUAL INTEGRATION IN THE FIGHTING FORCES OF THE UNITED STATES.
>
> An "all out" thundering march on Washington, ending in a monster and huge demonstration at Lincoln's Monument will shake up white America.

*Mrs. Eleanor Roosevelt, Fiorello H. LaGuardia and A. Philip Randolph
attending a rally in Madison Square Garden, February 1946.*
(AP/Bettmann)

It will shake up official Washington. . . .
It will gain respect for the Negro people.
It will create a new sense of self-respect among Negroes.

Randolph made the goals of the march very clear: By ending
discriminatory practices, thousands of jobs and hundreds of
millions of dollars in wages would be opened up for black
Americans, creating new industrial opportunities and providing hope for this segment of society.

"Most important and vital to all," Randolph's call reminded,
"Negroes, by the mobilization and coordination of their mass
power, can cause President Roosevelt to issue an executive
order abolishing discrimination in all government departments, army, navy, air corps, and national defense jobs."

President Roosevelt monitored Randolph's speeches and
plans and finally, made it clear to his staff that Randolph must
be talked out of the march. He sent a request to the two people

he called his "big guns"—Eleanor Roosevelt and Fiorello LaGuardia, the feisty popular mayor of New York City and a longtime friend to both Roosevelt and Randolph.

They met for a crucial discussion in an office in New York's City Hall on June 13, 1941. The First Lady made her position clear: "You know where I stand," she said and she emphasized her concern for the safety of the marchers. The nation's capitol city was still segregated along racial lines. The police force was white. Washington was largely a Jim Crow city and there were concerns, such as where the marchers would eat or sleep.

Courteous, polite but firm, Randolph emphasized that the march would not be called off unless the president issued an executive order banning discrimination in the defense industry.

An account of the meeting was given to President Roosevelt. Mayor LaGuardia suggested that the president might invite Randolph for another conference, and this advice was promptly followed.

On June 18, accompanied by Walter White, Randolph again faced Franklin Roosevelt. The president remained firm on some points. Forces of the Army and Navy would remain segregated, but the president did agree to set up a committee to investigate cases of discrimination in employment.

Randolph insisted that jobs were needed right now, not tomorrow or the day after.

Roosevelt and Randolph, two crafty leaders, bandied ideas back and forth. Finally, Roosevelt reportedly asked Randolph what he wanted him to do.

"We want something concrete," Randolph answered, "something tangible, definite, positive and affirmative," specifically, an order that abolished discrimination in war industries and in the armed forces.

Roosevelt hesitated; Randolph remained adamant. The president turned to Walter White asking the number of people expected to turn out for the march.

"One hundred thousand, Mr. President," Walter White answered with confidence.

President Roosevelt finally agreed that a committee would draft an Executive Order. Randolph made it clear that the march would not be called off until a satisfactory order was signed by the president.

Randolph monitored the drafting of the document until the wording met his satisfaction. Finally, on June 25, 1941, only six days before the scheduled march, Executive Order 8002, signed by President Roosevelt, became law.

Executive Order 8002 mandated that "there shall be no discrimination in the employment of workers in defense industries or government because of race, creed, color, or national origin." Furthermore, the new law stipulated that government agencies involved in defense or in production must "take special measures . . . to assure that such programs are administered without discrimination."

There was more. Under the new law, a Fair Employment Practices Committee (FEPC) was set up to investigate reported cases of discrimination and to arrange for solutions to legitimate complaints.

Under these new guidelines, many companies profiting from lucrative government contracts found it advantageous to begin hiring black workers. This change alone had far-reaching effects, opening job opportunities that had been closed to workers who were not of the white race.

Randolph realized the disappointment of thousands of his race who had planned and saved money for the Washington protest trip. The MOWM (March on Washington Movement) will continue, he promised. One day there will be a march.

To boost morale, Randolph took the lead in planning and coordinating gala programs held in selected large cities to celebrate the passage of Executive Order 8002. The rally in New York at Madison Square Garden on June 16, 1942, attracted the largest audience, more than 20,000. The cost of admission was kept low at only forty cents, allowing poor people to celebrate the new order and the anticipation of more social reforms that would follow.

The *Black Worker*, a journal edited by Randolph, headlined the celebration plans for Harlem. "Black Out Harlem June 16th," it informed the public.

Randolph used his artistic talents to help design leaflets for distribution to homes.

> Do you want work? Do you want equal rights?
> Do you want justice?
> Then prepare now to fight for it!

50,000 NEGROES MUST STORM MADISON SQUARE
GARDEN. MOBILIZE NOW!

The people came, filling Madison Square Garden. As Randolph was escorted into the auditorium, flanked by 100 Pullman porters in their uniforms and 50 Pullman maids forming a rear guard, the packed audience stood and cheered until Randolph finally held up his hands for silence.

The elaborate program of music and speeches kept the audience entertained for hours. Prominent black leaders gave speeches, taking advantage of the large audience. Always gallant, Randolph put aside the speech he had prepared, and gave the crowd the chance to listen to promising young black leaders such as Reverend Adam Clayton Powell, Jr., who in 1937 had officially succeeded his father as pastor of Harlem's Abyssinian Baptist Church, the largest Protestant congregation in the nation. That night in 1942 Powell rallied citizens to support his run to be the only black member of the United States House of Representatives.

Randolph also allowed other speakers to fill the hours. The joyous celebration reflected hope of new days dawning. The crusade for equal justice and full citizenship would continue. The MOWM had demonstrated a truth that would guide future planning: "POWER FLOWS FROM THE PEOPLE!"

2
LEGACY OF LEADERSHIP
1889–1911

"Gentle in nature, broad in vision, philosophical in thinking, devoted to his family . . . the Reverend James William Randolph . . . represented that sturdy, stable, old sterling fighting stock of the race in America. . . ."

—A. Philip Randolph

Whenever Asa Randolph reminisced about his childhood, his expressive voice and descriptive words made the Florida scenes so vivid that listeners could visualize the shifting events. He was proud of his name and the richness of his heritage. His father, a devout minister and a scholarly reader, introduced him at an early age to the great heroes of biblical history, including the hero whose name he gave his son.

As the African American Asa learned, the biblical Asa was born of royal heritage, son of Abijam, King of Judah, a kingdom in ancient Palestine, formed by the tribes of Judah and Benjamin after they broke with the other 10 tribes. According to the Bible, King Asa always tried to do what was right. Ruling over Judah from 915 to 875 B.C., he opposed the ancient practice of worshipping idols, the images looked upon as gods, and he ordered the removal of all the idols that had been introduced into the land of Judah. During his 41-year reign, King Asa brought peace to the Kingdom of Judah.

Asa Randolph, born in Crescent City, Florida, on April 15, 1889, was also destined to do what he believed was right. His father, James William Randolph, was born in 1864, the descendant of slaves who had been owned by members of the famous Randolph family of Virginia. (From the 1660s, Randolph statesmen can be traced in distinguished leadership roles. From William Randolph, a colonial administrator of Virginia and one of the founders of the College of William and Mary, the Randolph statesmen included governors, lawyers and stout-hearted statesmen who helped in shaping early America as a nation. According to customs and law, the slaves were considered the property of whomever owned them. The surname of the owner was often used to identify slaves as the "property of" and not as a relative.)

After President Lincoln issued the Emancipation Proclamation in 1863, most slaves who were set free had no money and no place to call home. Many slaves made their way to Florida, a beautiful state with a warm climate, undeveloped areas, a need for workers and a society not yet gripped by racial discrimination.

It was in Monticello, the capital city of Jefferson County, Florida, that Asa's father was born, one year after slavery ended. Monticello was known for the beauty of its broad streets, shaded by trees and well-built houses with yards enhanced by roses, camellias and other blooming plants.

Fortunately for some black children, many white missionaries from northern states had established schools and taught children of former slaves. James Randolph attended a school set up in Monticello by missionaries who were members of the Methodist church. Along with basic subjects, James mastered the skill of tailoring and also studied the Bible.

Inspired by the unselfish work of missionary teachers, James envisioned his life's work as a minister, teaching and preaching to descendants of former slaves, many of them groping their way through poverty. By the time he was twenty, he decided to become a traveling, or itinerant, preacher serving more than one church, often located in remote areas where people could not yet afford to pay a preacher, or to build a church. James Randolph was officially ordained as a minister of the African Methodist Episcopal (A.M.E.) church at that time. He became interested in Baldwin, a settlement in the northeastern section of Florida. Like most preachers in small rural communities, he served poor, isolated families.

Reverend Randolph was convinced to come to the lumbering town of Baldwin by James and Mary Robinson, who had moved there with their four daughters. Baldwin's population of around 400 was equally divided along racial lines, and jobs were plentiful because workers were needed to haul lumber and cut wood used by paper mills, and to help lay railroad cross-ties.

At an intersection where two dirt roads crossed in Baldwin stood the small wooden Campbell A.M.E. Chapel. The membership of about 50 persons looked forward to the first and third Sundays of each month when young Reverend Randolph came to preach. Most members spent the entire day at church, beginning with Sunday School and ending with evening services.

The young preacher frequently visited the log cabin home of the Robinson family, who lived two miles from the church. Each Sunday when Reverend Randolph preached, he knew that Mary Robinson and her four daughters would, like many families who traveled long distances, bring enough food for the entire day.

Mary Robinson's husband, James, supported his family by buying and selling lumber, and raising hogs to cure and sell as bacon. The four Robinson daughters—Mattie, Esther, Carne and Elizabeth—always came with their mother to Sunday School and church services. Most families in the area were poor, many were newcomers to Florida, and traveling ministers received no set salaries from the small churches they served. Families who had no money to give would bring gifts of food such as chickens, ham, potatoes, vegetables from their gardens and preserves—whatever the families felt the minister would appreciate. Churchgoers who were too poor to give anything tangible offered their sincere thanks and prayers.

The friendship between the young minister and the Robinson family deepened with each passing year. In time, it was the family's youngest daughter who captured his heart. A teenager with striking beauty and a stately figure, Elizabeth shared the minister's affection and became his wife in 1885. It was quite common during this period for young girls to marry and begin raising a family while still in their teens.

Two years later, the couple's first son was born and named James William Randolph, Jr. A short time after his birth

Reverend Randolph moved his family to Crescent City, Florida, an expanding community that offered him an opportunity to serve a large congregation. It was in Crescent City that their second child was born, the son they named Asa. By the time Asa was two years old, Reverend Randolph knew the time had come to move on to a still larger city, one with greater opportunities for his two sons.

He accepted an invitation to preach in Jacksonville, Florida, and in 1891, the minister, his wife and two young sons moved to Florida's capital city, located on the beautiful St. Johns River. The bustling seaport was rapidly growing in population and commerce. Orange trees were being planted. Railroads were expanding to transport the hundreds of tourists and workers who were attracted to the city by its climate, beauty and opportunities for work. At the time the Randolph family arrived, the population of Jacksonville was divided almost equally between white and black families. Rigid lines of racial segregation were rapidly forming, however, as newcomers crowded the city.

In bustling Jacksonville, the Randolph family rented a neat two-story house in a section where the population was racially mixed. However, as more white families moved into the city, more and more black families were being crowded into racially segregated sections.

The house rented by Reverend Randolph was old but comfortable. The two growing boys enjoyed the wide front porch, the yard circled by a picket fence and the shade of two oak trees towering like sentinels at the front gate. The spacious yard had places to plant flowers and a vegetable garden. Inside the house, an old-fashioned fireplace kept the rooms warm on cold evenings. Upstairs, a kerosene heater was sufficient to keep the bedrooms warm if winter evenings grew chilly.

Long before James and Asa began formal schooling, Reverend Randolph nourished their inquisitive minds by reading aloud to them every day. An avid reader himself, the minister began assembling a small home library by purchasing some of his favorite classics, book by book. In his expressive speaking style, refined to deliver sermons, he read from the works of Charles Dickens, Shakespeare, John Keats and other outstanding writers. The Bible remained a mainstay for their

Air view of Jacksonville, Florida, in the 1920s. (UPI/Bettmann)

read-aloud sessions, for discussions and for memorizing passages.

Asa and James learned from their father the history of courageous heroes of the African-American race, particularly those in the ministry. The two boys learned how Reverend Richard Allen, born a plantation slave in 1760 and later sold to a Delaware planter, worked and earned money to buy his own freedom. In bondage, Richard Allen had read and preached to other slaves. In freedom, he settled in Philadelphia and attended a Methodist Episcopal Church. Outraged that African Americans were forced to worship apart from white congregations, he organized what later became the African Methodist Episcopal Church.

In Jacksonville, Asa's father took him to meet the famous Bishop Henry MacNeal Turner at a church convention. The young boy learned how Bishop Turner had taught himself to read and write by studying the Bible and hymn books. During the Civil War, Turner became the first African American to be commissioned as an army chaplain and, after the war, he was elected to the Georgia legislature and became known for his compassionate fight for the welfare of both black and white workers.

Bishop Turner's bold actions and brilliant speeches gave courage to his race. When asked how he remained fearless and continued to protest racism in the face of threats upon his life, Turner arched his bushy eyebrows, held up his Bible, brandished his pistols, then gave his answer: "My life depends upon the will of God and these two guns." The bishop's courage and fights for justice impressed Randolph and helped to shape him during his maturing years.

Jim Crow customs eventually changed to fixed racist laws in states of the Deep South. Jacksonville became known as a "one hundred percent cracker town," meaning it was rigidly segregated and racist.

Determined that his sons would not be cowed by racist laws, Reverend Randolph set up his own rules to guide their actions. They were not to sit in segregated rooms, nor were the boys permitted to ride the Jim Crow streetcar. They walked wherever they went.

Asa and James walked to the all black public school with classes from first through the fifth grade. Many educators in Deep South states reasoned that any job available to students of color should not require learning beyond that level.

Reverend Randolph trained his sons to prepare for a different America where racism did not control decisions. Fortunately, Cookman Institute had been founded in Jacksonville in 1807 under the Freedmen's Bureau, the agency set up by the United States Congress to help former slaves establish their lives as free persons. After the Civil War ended, the Freedman's Bureau and the American Missionary Association worked together to maintain schools to teach the children of former slaves who otherwise would have received only a meager education, if any. Compassionate white teachers gave the students a rich and broad educational background, knowing that few would be able to work their way through college. Training in trades was available because most students usually became workers immediately after they left Cookman.

Asa and his brother had grown up with the understanding that they would work to help with their personal and school expenses. In the city of Jacksonville, however, the work being offered to young black people was chiefly menial and low paying. Asa and James tried an assortment of jobs. They sold newspapers in downtown Jacksonville and ran errands for neighbors. They assisted with the dry cleaning business set up by their mother in the backyard of their home. Much of the time, their father was kept busy conducting church services, visiting sick parishioners, helping families with funeral arrangements and tending to other needs of his congregation .

As Asa's body grew to six feet, he tried laborious work that usually earned a little more money. He worked as helper to a grocery store owner after school hours, stopping home only long enough to pick up his dinner to eat later. One summer he even worked as a section hand on the railroad, helping to lay cross-ties and rails.

Work never interfered with studies in the Randolph family. Both Asa and James excelled in all their subjects, including Latin, philosophy and the sciences. Under the guidance of Cookman teachers, many of them scholars from New England, the two brothers developed into excellent students.

Asa and James seemed to excel in any aspect of school life they chose to pursue. Asa's baritone voice won a prominent place in the school choir. On the school's baseball team, he became an expert catcher, as well as a first baseman. A schoolmate pondered in later years that Randolph "could have made a career as a baseball player." He was equally gifted in basketball. Others who listened to young Asa sing or watched his movements and heard his impeccable phrasings predicted his fame as a performer.

Despite his popularity and abilities, Asa remained somewhat shy and reserved. He would praise his brother who, in his reserved manner, was equally gifted and scholarly. The two brothers motivated and encouraged one another in the way their father had trained them to do.

In scholarship, Asa and James remained a whisper apart in grade points. At their graduation exercises in 1907, Asa delivered the valedictorian address that he titled "The Man of the Hour." When asked about the title in later years, Randolph recalled that his speech gave his view of "what I would like to see young Negroes do."

On the morning after graduation, Asa began searching for a full-time job. As he well knew, the racial relationships between white and black citizens of Jacksonville had changed since his childhood days. After the disastrous fire of 1901 destroyed sections of the city, many neighborhoods had become more aligned along racial lines. As more and more black citizens came looking for work in the rapidly developing city, the neighborhoods formed along even more strict racial lines.

In this more restrictive racial climate, it was difficult even for a brilliant young native to secure a well-paying employment. Asa tried an assortment of jobs available to members of his race. All were low-paying; most were laborious. For a time, Asa worked as an insurance collector, collecting dues by going door-to-door as was the custom. He also returned to briefly helping to lay railroad tracks. He shoveled coal.

Meanwhile, Asa Randolph pondered his future. He had demonstrated that he possessed many talents, but in the restrictive segregated atmosphere of the South he did not feel challenged. Frustrated, he reached the decision being made by thousands of young people of his race who had brilliant minds, multiple skills and willingness to work, but whose aspirations locked in a dead-end path by "segregation" or "Jim Crow."

Like thousands of black citizens across America, Asa Randolph refused to be caged into that future. In April, 1911, he left Jacksonville for New York in search of new opportunities. Traveling with him was a close friend, Beaman Hearn, who promised his parents to return at summer's end.

Asa gave no promises; he traveled in search of his future. He became part of the first wave of the "Great Migration" of African Americans who came from states of the Deep South, hoping to find in New York direction for their lives and talents. For Asa, as for many others, the destination was Harlem.

3

NEW YORK YEARS
1911–1916

"If the problems of race and color are hard
in the United States, so be it; let us not lose
heart and run away from them, but gird to
solve them."

—A. Philip Randolph

It was springtime in 1911 when Asa Randolph and Beaman
Hearn arrived in the section of Manhattan Island known
as Harlem. By this time its population changed from Dutch
to Irish to Jewish to Negro.

From their rented room in an attractive house located between Seventh and Lenox Avenues, the twenty-two-year-old
Florida friends were contrasts in appearance and personality.
Hearn was short and stout in stature. Randolph had a lean
figure that had stretched to over six feet in height. His neat,
well-tailored outfits reflected his mother's skill and the pride
he took in his appearance. Beaman Hearn wanted only to enjoy
the sights of New York. Randolph also came to Harlem to see
the sights, but he sought new directions for his life as well.

The two friends found cheap lodging. A relative of Hearn's
had secured a room for only $1.50 a week in a home on 132nd
Street. Settled, Randolph began exploring the section of New
York that would come to be known as "Black Manhattan" in
the book (of the same name) written by James Weldon Johnson,
published in 1930. Johnson described Harlem as "a black city,
located in the heart of white Manhattan, and containing more
Negroes to the square mile than any spot on earth." In 1911
when Randolph arrived, the population of black citizens in all

the boroughs in New York City was 91,709; in Manhattan alone, it was 60,534.

Other waves of black newcomers were yet to come.

So was the racial climate in Manhattan when three black businessmen—Philip A. Payton, J.C. Thomas and John B. Nail—purchased rows of large apartment buildings and rented to black tenants. A church with a wealthy congregation bought a row of apartments. The buying and speculating continued. Realtors bought and sold. Poor people saved until they had enough funds for loans or mortgages.

Philip A. Payton persuaded white realtors to rent vacant apartments on Fifth Avenue to waiting black tenants. White homeowners tried to halt the trend of buying, but the need for homes was too strong. For the first time in their lives, hundreds of black citizens had the chance to buy the kind of homes in which they had worked as cooks or maids, but never dreamed of owning. Suddenly, with a company owned by black realtors, these citizens could buy on terms that made monthly payments possible.

In *Black Manhattan*, James Weldon Johnson recorded the response of wealthy white homeowners. "They took flight, they became panic-stricken. Their conduct could be compared to that of a community in the Middle Ages fleeing before an epidemic of the black plague. . . . The stampeding whites deserted house after house and block after block. Then prices dropped . . . lower than the bottom."

Coinciding with this event was the outbreak of World War I in Europe and the unprecedented labor shortage as the United States tried to furnish munitions and supplies to countries at war. Labor agents went South and arranged transportation for workers willing to travel North, sometimes as many as 2,500 in a single day. As Johnson recalled, "The exodus was on." A similar exodus took place from the West Indies.

Newcomers of both groups readily found well-paying jobs and took advantage of the prices of Harlem homes that continued to drop. As Johnson noted, "Harlem was taken over without violence." For newcomers from the Deep South states, New York's Harlem seemed the "Promised Land" compared to the hardships they left behind.

By the time Asa Randolph arrived, new apartment houses had been built in West Harlem along Seventh and Lenox

Avenues. Black citizens were then living chiefly between 128th and 145th Streets, with Fifth Avenue and Seventh Avenue forming a separating boundary for white dwellers.

From the beginning, Harlem fascinated Randolph. He spent his first days exploring the sights and learning Harlem's unusual history. The more he learned, the better he would understand the things he saw and heard in one of the most unique sections of America. James Weldon Johnson would later share his similar fascination with Harlem in *Black Manhattan*. Asa Randolph used the sights and sounds and history of Manhattan as a fascinating learning adventure, not fully realizing that the direction of his own life would be shaped by it.

Asa's first Harlem experiences were more as a tourist, taking in glimpses of the signs of poverty, the crowded apartment buildings and the racial separation nearly as obvious as that of Deep South cities. Accustomed to walking rather than riding on segregated Jacksonville transportation, he began exploring on foot the section described by Johnson as a "city within a city" providing black Americans with "better, cleaner, more modern, more airy, more sunny homes than they ever lived in before."

Johnson rightfully gave great credit for this historic change to Philip A. Payton, Jr., a black realtor who graduated from college, but was forced to work at such jobs as handyman and barber after earning his degree. He became interested in real estate while working as a janitor for realtors, and began studying until he became a realtor himself, advertising as "Agent and Broker, 67 West 134th Street." By the time Randolph arrived in Harlem, Payton had become the most prosperous realtor in the city.

Churches began following the movements of their members. Salem Memorial Mission, founded by Reverend F.A. Cullen (adopted father of the popular poet, Countee Cullen), moved into the building vacated by a white congregation. Churches of other denominations also moved, buying other buildings as white congregations left Harlem. Within 10 years after Randolph's arrival, the majority of established churches with all-black memberships were located in Harlem. "On to Harlem" movements motivated most churches to move or begin planning to move. Churches with prosperous members invested in homes as well.

As Randolph became acquainted with Harlem, each day of exploration deepened his fascination for its diversities and possibilities, and also for its needs. Before looking for his niche, however, he spent weeks studying and enjoying the things that made Harlem so special.

Each morning he dressed early, taking care that his attire was neat and well coordinated. After a leisurely breakfast at an inexpensive restaurant at 130th Street and Lenox Avenue, he was ready for adventure. Some days it would be the popular Hippodrome Theater at 44th Street and Sixth Avenue, where admittance was only twenty-five cents and he could stay as long as he desired. Randolph had not yet completely given up his interest in using his voice in a theatrical career.

On many days, Randolph spent the hours strolling the shaded streets of Harlem that had not yet become over-crowded. Other waves of newcomers were yet to come.

At summer's end, Beaman Hearn kept his promise and returned to Jacksonville. Randolph decided that for the present, he would remain in Harlem and find direction for his life. He was still uncertain which of his talents would receive major emphasis—a stage career as an actor, a baseball player or a singer, perhaps alone or in a quartet or a chorus.

Out of money, he looked for work and discovered that in Harlem most of the jobs offered to black workers were the same types as those offered in Jacksonville—laborious, low-paying, boring, without permanency. Having little choice, Randolph began accepting jobs, but worked only until he had saved enough money to last for a few weeks. As he explained, "the jobs Negroes could get weren't worth spending much time on."

One of his first jobs was that of elevator operator. As Paul Lawrence Dunbar had noted, this was one of the low-paying jobs usually offered to black males. Dunbar wrote some of his first poems while he worked as an elevator operator in his hometown of Dayton, Ohio. Randolph learned later of Dunbar's readings in Manhattan, and of his writing lyrics for productions by Jacksonville's Johnson Brothers and Will Marion Cook. As Dunbar had written poetry during the monotonous work, Randolph read and began to plot his future in Harlem. He knew that without further studies, as a black man the low-paying, menial jobs would be what he could expect in the future.

Randolph also turned to the church, which had always been a part of his life as well as a place for newcomers to make friends and wholesome social contacts. He chose Salem Methodist Church, that was located on West 133rd Street. The pastor was Reverend Frederick Cullen.

Salem had started a number of youth groups, including one called the Epworth League, organized to study the Bible. By the time Randolph joined, the League had also organized a theater club. The young people who acted out the plays were amateurs, but took their roles seriously and presented performances for community audiences. Randolph willingly used this chance to star in such plays as "Othello," "Hamlet," and "The Merchant of Venice," memorizing every line from each of the dramas in which he acted. His practice and performances gave his speech pattern a recognizable distinction.

It was through John Ramsey, a club member, that Randolph learned about opportunities at City College. Ramsey's appearance was that of a very poor young man, yet he attended the college. One day Randolph took courage and asked him about his schooling. Ramsey's reply changed the direction of Randolph's future. A student could attend the City College of New York without paying a lot of money, he learned. Randolph had a good scholastic record, and he, too, could attend.

He promptly applied for admittance. The excellent grades from Cookman Institute were accepted. The following February, Randolph registered as a student of City College and began his studies with classes in public speaking.

One Sunday afternoon as he performed with the Salem group, he noticed that Henri Strange, a performer on the Harlem stage, watched him intently. A few days later as Randolph ate in a luncheonette on Lenox Avenue, Strange entered, sat at Randolph's table and began chatting. He complimented Randolph on his performances and offered him a place in his drama group.

At last, a professional stage career was Randolph's for the taking! He immediately wrote a joyful letter to his parents in Jacksonville, sharing the good news. Their response was immediate, but hope-shattering. If he wanted to seek his future in New York, they understood. But never, they told their son, could they approve of his spending a life on the stage—not in New York. Many parents viewed such careers as too worldly and fraught with temptations. Disappointed, but respecting his parents' wishes, Randolph turned away from the opportunity to gain fame.

Facing a crossroads in his life, Randolph halted studies at City College and enrolled as an evening student at NYU. His studies included economy, philosophy and social sciences. Many of the evening students, he soon learned, were brilliant thinkers. Racial differences did not mark dividing lines in these classrooms as in many other areas of society. The learning atmosphere was rich with discussions between the students and with their professors.

Equally important as class sessions were discussion groups that formed after the classes ended. Students debated relevant topics, such as ways to improve America's economy, problems in politics and general social, economic and political issues. Primary to most discussion sessions was the great need for social change that eventually would bring economic improvement.

Randolph's learning was enriched by his visits to an elegant structure designed in white Vermont marble and located between Fortieth and Forty-second Streets. This central building of the New York Public Library had reopened for service on May 3, 1911, after being closed for complete renovation. The main reading room of the new structure covered half an acre. Like most new patrons, Randolph became intrigued by the building and even more excited about the learning treasures it housed.

Many other students at New York University shared Randolph's love for the library and his idea that socialism would help black American citizens achieve greater and more immediate racial equality. The drawback, however, was the refusal of most labor unions to admit black workers as members. Randolph began to better understand how deep-seated racial prejudice formed barriers and blocked attempts to bring together all American workers as a unified group to work for the elimination of the problems that blocked the paths to progressive improvements.

Randolph redirected his interest to political issues. During the years 1912 to 1914, students at City College gathered together to discuss the revolutionary changes taking place in America, particularly among the black Americans. The mass migration to cities of the South and West continued to bring changes in lives of Americans, particularly those of the black race. Voices of protest and demands for reforms gave promise of a new world order where skin color was merely a mark of heredity, not of worth or future accomplishments. As Randolph and other newcomers discovered, life in Harlem was not always easy or free of problems. It was, however, always alive with fun and full of hope. Students of City College illustrated their hope in the future by taking actions such as holding rallies and collecting funds to help textile workers who were on strike in Massachusetts and New Jersey.

As Randolph and other NYU students engaged in discussions after classes, he became more interested in problems affecting Americans, especially those who were poor. He had problems of his own, but it was his nature to worry more about the sufferings of others. Schoolmates knew he was sometimes without food, yet he would be worrying about the other people of the world who were hungry.

Like many other students at NYU, Asa Randolph became fascinated by the writings and teachings of Karl Marx, the economist, writer and philosopher credited as the "Father of Communism." Born May 5, 1818, in Trier, Germany, Marx wrote many of the theories of modern communism and socialism.

Motivated by discussions with other college students studying sociology, Randolph began to study theories of communism, which he saw as a possible means of helping members of his race who, by necessity, would have to be underpaid laborers. The theories of Karl Marx and of socialism were provoking many young Americans to question the capitalist system in American society.

The writings of Marx changed Randolph's thinking about his own future pursuits, and the possibilities for those of his race. In his writings, Marx considered the plight of the working people whose toil produced most of the goods sold. But it was the capitalists, not the workers, who received most of the profits. Collaborating with his friend, Friedrich Engels, Marx co-authored the "Communist Manifesto," a famous program which urged the workers—the *proletariat*—to revolt and establish a planned economic system in which the government would own all property. Workers would then get a more equitable reward for their efforts.

Reasoning that descendants of slaves would no doubt remain a significant majority of the workers, Randolph began concentrating upon ways to improve working conditions in Harlem and throughout the nation. To debate such issues, he organized a discussion group known as the New York Independent Political Council. Black students at New York University joined the council, participated enthusiastically in the discussion groups and later broadened the council to include debates in local churches.

It was at one of the Independent Political Council debates that Randolph made the acquaintance of Ernest Welcome, a young man who had opened an employment agency, the Brotherhood of Labor in New York. The Brotherhood guided newcomers to Harlem in locating and holding jobs. Most of the clients came from the nation's southern states, or from the West Indies. Welcome persuaded Randolph to assist him with the project and use his artistic talents to design instructional pamphlets that the clients would need.

The chance to help job seekers was a welcome assignment. Randolph used the experiences of his early weeks in Harlem to help the newcomers to find and keep jobs. To help the business prosper, he designed colorful posters for publicity and to provide specific directions for clients not yet familiar with Harlem's layout.

Soon job seekers, desperate for work, began crowding the agency. Randolph not only placed them in jobs, but he also trained them in skills and attitudes needed for success. His own difficulty in finding acceptable work helped him to understand the plight of black job seekers. This experience deepened his interest in workers and the problems they faced.

Work in the job bureau also directed Randolph's life toward a totally new interest. Each day as he walked to his office, he passed a beauty parlor and saw women entering and then later leaving with handsome hairstyles. One day he met the slender, shapely woman who ran the enterprise. With a captivating smile, she introduced herself as Lucille Campbell Green, manager of the beauty salon.

From that first meeting, Lucille Green and Asa Randolph established a firm friendship. Until he met Lucille, Randolph had devoted his time chiefly to civil rights issues and to his studies. Now, suddenly, he was smitten. The fact that she was five years older than Randolph made no difference to him.

Within a few days, the two were enjoying dinner dates and taking long walks. Lucille shared facts about her early life in Virginia and her college career at Howard University in Washington, D.C., where she earned certification as a teacher. After graduation from Howard, she married a schoolmate, Joseph Green, who had studied law, and the couple moved to New York City. Lucille began teaching school. Her husband found employment as a customs officer, but died after a brief illness. Distraught and lonely, Lucille changed her career and began studying the new hair-styling system made famous by Madam C. J. Walker.

Randolph knew Madam Walker and her life story. Born Sarah Williams, the child of ex-slaves, she took in washing to make a living. Wanting a home of her own, she married Moses McWilliams, and in 1885, a daughter, A'Lelia, was born. After her husband died, Sarah moved to St. Louis, Missouri, determined to give her daughter a good education.

One night, Sarah listened to an inspiring speech by Margaret Murray Washington, wife of Booker T. Washington, who challenged women of her race to improve their lives. Inspired, Sarah continued her experimentation with a formula that could change the texture of hair. The formula became so successful that she soon began to establish schools to educate beauticians in using it.

After Sarah married Charles Joseph Walker in 1906, she began using the name Madam C. J. Walker. When A'Lelia graduated from college, the two women began establishing schools of beauty to teach the use of Madam Walker's products and techniques. Madam Walker donated a large portion of her fortune to colleges such as Tuskegee Institute and Bethune Cookman College, as well as other charitable organizations. Lucille Green was a close friend to A'Lelia Walker, and that is how she became involved in the beauty salon business.

Lucile soon fell in love with Asa Randolph. The attraction became mutual. Usually shy with women, Randolph seemed to feel at home with the vivacious beautician. The friendship surprised many people who knew the couple. Lucille Green's outgoing personality seemed in sharp contrast to Randolph's formal, always polite manner. Yet they shared a kinship, a passion for helping anyone in need. Lucille's friends recalled how she would give away things she needed "if she thought you needed them more." Randolph's friends often paid him a similar compliment, saying that "he would give you the shirt off his back."

Randolph accompanied Lucille to meetings and entertainments at Madam Walker's fashionable town house on 135th Street in Harlem. Other times, the elaborate parties and picnics were given at Villa Lewaro, the stunning mansion Madam Walker built on the east bank of New York's Hudson River. The mansion's name was formed from the first two letters of A'Lelia's names—Lelia Walker Robinson, LEWARO. The elaborate home also became a gathering place for serious civil rights discussions and planning.

Lucille Green and Asa Randolph were married in November 1914. Randolph honored his bride's wishes for a wedding at St. Philip's Episcopal Church in Harlem where Lucille was a longtime member. Typically thoughtful, Lucille gave her new husband the pleasure of choosing their honeymoon trip. True to his no-frills nature, Randolph chose a long streetcar ride down to the tip end of Manhattan and back. Lucille enjoyed the "honeymoon trip" and began adjusting to the lifestyle of her "Buddy," their affectionate name for each other.

It was at one of Madam Walker's parties that Lucille introduced Randolph to Chandler Owen, a scholarly, fast-talking young man with large penetrating eyes, an upturned nose and a brilliant mind. From their first meeting, Owen and Randolph formed a close friendship. Both were interested in scholarly studies and they shared a consuming passion to elevate African Americans to higher living standards, economically and socially. The two friends began calling each other "Boy," a term frequently used in southern states to symbolize closeness and caring.

Both progressive thinkers, Owen and Randolph concluded that socialism offered the best solutions to the problems in America. The more that Randolph and Owen learned about socialism, the more they were convinced that it offered the route that might take their race toward social and political equality.

Many evenings after studies at NYU, Randolph joined interested students in debating the theories of labor leaders, including Eugene Debs, who called for reforms that would give more consideration to workers who helped to produce goods that made a few persons wealthy. An advocate of socialism, Debs had been sentenced to 10 years in jail in 1918 for speaking out against American participation in World War I.

Asa Randolph became especially engrossed in the theories of Debs, who organized the Socialist Party in 1901 and the Industrial Workers of the World in 1905. (His interest in reforms for workers became well known when he ran as a presidential candidate in 1900, 1904, 1908, 1912 and 1920, where he won six percent of the popular vote.) Born in Terre Haute, Indiana, in 1855, Debs went to work on the railroads at age fourteen, and later formed the American Railway Union (A.R.U.) in 1893, which took part in the Pullman strike the following year. The strike was broken by federal troops.

Whenever Eugene Debs was scheduled to give a speech in New York, Randolph and Owen arranged to attend. Debs voiced compassion for the plight of African Americans and for all the poor working people who were at the mercy of wealthy bosses. Randolph praised Debs, noting his exceptional spiritual character.

The philosophy of socialism intrigued both Owen and Randolph. The concept of the distribution of goods and wealth being shared by workers whose labor helped to produce the wealth would benefit African Americans, especially those of the working class.

Another prominent socialist speaker who held Randolph's rapt attention was Hubert H. Harrison, a Virgin Islander who migrated to the United States. An expert in African history, he conducted lectures from street corners, more frequently from the corner of 135th Street and Lenox Avenue, a spot he called his "outdoor university." Black speakers frequently used that popular street corner to teach or to publicize messages, speeches, upcoming events—any information electronic devices can now transmit.

Randolph listened to Harrison's powerful voice as he explained to listeners how socialism could help workers of their race improve the levels of their living. Soon Randolph became a soapbox orator while others crowded to hear his message on socialism. This technique of soapbox oratory is believed by some people to have been invented by the ex-slave Frederick Douglass, who used his magnificent speaking voice to preach for an end to the slave system. Because African American orators were not usually permitted to occupy the same podium as white speakers, Douglass began giving orations by standing on a box at a prominent street corner. Listeners came and Douglass was heard.

And Asa Randolph was heard. A box was not always needed. The street-corner orator simply stood and began his message. At some point, the original speaker might stop and give his speaking spot over to a colleague. Chandler Owen usually knew precisely when it was time for him to take over the corner and relieve Randolph.

In their speeches, the two young orators urged listeners to consider that the Socialist party encouraged African Americans to become members, while most other political parties were paying little attention to the problems they faced.

In his speeches, Randolph never tried to arouse anger or hatred. Instead, he shared ideas and inspired the listeners to think. An admiring listener remarked that Randolph just seemed to carry the young people in his palms. Other listeners marveled how his vibrant voice held listeners spellbound.

So, on a street corner of Harlem, Randolph discovered new avenues for his talents. He quickly became one of the most popular soapbox orators of the time. He needed no props and no special introductions, but used a box as his stage, or simply stood at the corner and began to speak. One person would stop to listen, then another, until a crowd formed a listening audience. Randolph's commanding appearance and voice seemed to always attract a crowd.

Randolph and Chandler Owen became so engrossed in socialism and soapbox speaking that they deferred their college studies. They spent most of their time learning about socialism and making speeches to teach the concept to their listening audiences. Under socialism, citizens could be guaranteed such rights as social justice, equality and individual freedom. This system, socialist leaders believed, could help to solve problems of industrial society such as unemployment, poverty and conflicts between business and labor.

By 1916, both friends decided to join the Socialist Party, and Randolph settled on the directions his talents should take him. The group to receive his primary focus, he believed, should be the workers, especially those who were poor and powerless. In America, this would include a major portion of his race, many of them forming the first generation of their families who could live and work in freedom.

For these people, Randolph mounted his soapbox nightly and raised his sonorous voice, the voice that his father thought would deliver sermons in a grand church. For workers of his race, for workers of all races, Randolph preached commanding advice from his street-corner pulpit: "Organize! Organize!"

4

MOVEMENTS AND THE MESSENGER 1917–1924

"Finally, a new Negro arrived on the scene at the time of all other forward, aggressive groups and movements. . . . He is the product of the same worldwide forces that brought into being the great liberal and radical movements that are seizing the reins of political and social powers in the civilized countries of the world."

—The Editors of the *Messenger*, 1920

The year 1917 marked revolutionary changes for the United States and for Asa Randolph. In April, 1917, United States President Woodrow Wilson issued a declaration of war against Germany, despite his promise to keep the United States out of World War I.

Seven months later, Randolph announced the advent of the *Messenger*, a monthly magazine to bring "light and learning to the world." With Chandler Owen as co-editor, the pages of the new publication offered news and comments to evoke the light and learning it promised. Priced at fifteen cents, for the times slightly higher than most magazines that cost no more than ten cents, the bold print beneath the title of the *Messenger* proclaimed: "The Only Radical Negro Magazine in America."

The contents page of the new magazine was neatly laid out with the names of the two editors given equal billing: A. Philip Randolph, President—Chandler Owen, Secretary-Treasurer. The contents were outlined under seven subject categories:

1) Editorials;
2) Economics and Politics;
3) Education and Literature;
4) Poets' Corner;
5) Theater-Drama-Music;
6) Messages From the *Messenger*; and
7) Who's Who.

With almost no money and with credit from a Brooklyn printer, the *Messenger* was launched. For office space, editors used two very small rooms on the third floor of a brownstone house in Harlem. They worked on a second-hand desk and wrote their columns on a battered typewriter in a room that was cramped and cluttered. Nevertheless, when copies of the new periodicals were publicized, the magazine quickly gained subscribers. Sales increased each month as readers looked forward to what the two editors and their guest writers had to say.

During the first months of publication, the *Messenger* consumed much of Randolph's time. Finances remained a major problem and the publishing budget operated on the edge. Fortunately for the publishers, most of the writers who contributed articles to the fledgling journal had visions of later becoming publishers themselves and shared Randolph's militant attitude concerning the urgency for reforms regarding jobs and full citizenship rights for all Americans. Many writers contributed articles, stories or poems and asked for no payment. They were happy to see their writing in print.

By November, 1917, when the first copy of the *Messenger* was published, America's President Woodrow Wilson had already asked Congress for a declaration of war against Germany. "We are but one of the champions of the rights of mankind," the president told citizens as he explained why the nation was entering the conflict in Europe. Randolph and Owen challenged the president in the *Messenger*, citing lynching, Jim Crow, segregation, discrimination inside the armed forces and in society, and disfranchisement of millions of black souls in the South. All these things, they reminded the president, "make your cry of making the world safe for democracy a sham, a mockery, a rape of decency and a travesty on common justice."

Years of study and thinking had clarified Randolph's views of many subjects. By 1917, as a socialist, he believed that the

European conflict would be of almost no benefit to the workers of the world and, therefore, he advised members of his race to resist the draft and confine their efforts to reforms needed on the home front.

With a bold announcement that the *Messenger* would be orientated toward socialism, Randolph and Owen let it be known that the publication might seem radical in tone, defining radicals as those who seek to get at the root of the world's problems. The editors also assured the public that, "We shall interpret social policies and economic conditions, municipal, state, national, and international, with calm, dispassionate poise."

As World War I escalated, Dr. W. E. B. DuBois, who for years had been praised for his inspiration in modern protest movements, published an editorial in the *Crisis*, the NAACP journal which he edited, advising his race: "Let us, while the war lasts, forget our special grievances and close our ranks shoulder to shoulder with our own white fellow citizens. We make no ordinary sacrifice, but let us make it gladly and willingly with our eyes lifted to the hills."

Randolph and Owen offered a different view of the war and the certain loss of lives. Through the voice of the *Messenger*, they advised readers that the thinking of many black citizens had changed and that "their gospel of obey and trust has been replaced by one of rebel and demand. . . ."

Despite their difference on the war issue, Randolph admired DuBois for his brilliance as an editor and writer, and also for what he termed "his adherence to the fine manners of his background." On the issues of segregation and war, however, Randolph refused to compromise with anyone, and a *Messenger* article stated his thinking that "no intelligent Negro is willing to lay down his life for the United States as it now exists."

In the *Messenger* for November, 1917, the two editors signed an invitation "To Our Readers" stating that "The *Messenger's* forum is open to its readers. Manuscripts of articles, poems and short stories are solicited."

One feature of high interest in that November issue was headlined by the name in bold letters of "MORRIS HILLQUIT," a candidate for President of the United States in the upcoming national election. The credentials of the candidate were neatly outlined:

"Morris Hillquit represents the working people and 90%
of the Negroes are working people. Morris Hillquit
is a Jew, born in Russia. . . ."

Randolph added his printed comments in the *Messenger*
stating that "Hillquit believes the war is over the exploitation
of the darker people. . . . He is the only candidate who dares to
say so." A large photograph of Hillquit highlighted his handsome features that had become familiar to the American public.

Another page featured an article on black soldiers, noting
that Negroes were probably "the best and most loyal troops in
the United States. But the government has failed too often to
do its duties by the Negro solider."

Still another article was headlined by a single word in bold
letters: "PEACE." Readers were reminded that "If only half the
billions which have been expended in this war had been expended on education, men would not now be killing one another
because they were born on a different strip of land. Peace would
be nearer at hand, and we want peace."

Randolph realized the risk of making his statements against
the war. The Espionage Act passed by Congress in June, 1917,
gave the government power to ban newspapers from the mail,
and to punish with fines and imprisonment anyone found
guilty of making antiwar speeches.

In the summer of 1918, the two *Messenger* editors planned a
tour of large American cities to give speeches against war and,
at the same time, teach members of their race about the
socialist movements. The first city visited was Cleveland, Ohio,
where they had been invited to speak and to bring copies of the
Messenger to be sold during the meetings.

Randolph and Owen took off for the tour, even though the
Espionage Act had now been amended to give the government
power to punish anyone found guilty of obstructing conscription.

On the evening of August 4, the *Messenger* editors spoke to
a large crowd gathered at a street corner in Cleveland. They
advised listeners to resist going to war and to fight at home.
As requested, copies of the *Messenger* were being sold to the
crowd.

An agent of the Justice Department purchased a copy and listened to Randolph's speech. He then took both Randolph and Owen into custody for further investigation.

On their return to New York in mid-August, the two editors were informed by the Postmaster General that the *Messenger* would no longer be given second-class mailing privileges. More unsettling news followed. Chandler Owen was drafted into the army and sent to a camp in the South for training. Randolph also received an induction notice informing him that he would be drafted into the armed services in November. Two days after he received the notice, the armistice with Germany and Austria-Hungary was declared. Randolph was no doubt saved from a long prison confinement.

More problems awaited the two *Messenger* editors after the war, however. The Postmaster General, Albert Burleson, refused to continue second-class mailing privileges for the *Messenger*. As Randolph described the dilemma, "Burleson threw the *Messenger* out of the mails."

During and after World War I, a series of race riots had erupted in the United States, in the North and South. Many riots involved black soldiers. The sight of black soldiers dressed in military uniforms seemed to evoke outrage and hatred from white citizens in several cities. Violence against black citizens began intensifying by 1917, causing a torrent of attacks by white mobs in several sections of the nation, particularly in sections of the South where large numbers of blacks were lynched. This violence continued after the war ended.

Lynching was documented in the book *The Voice of the Negro*, edited by Robert T. Kerlin, professor of English at Virginia Military Institute, and includes a compilation of lynchings during the year 1919 alone. The book was forwarded upon request to Robert R. Moton, then the head of Tuskegee Institute. The summary of the report by states read: Alabama—7; Arkansas—12; Colorado—2; Florida—5; Georgia—21; Louisiana—7; Mississippi—12; Missouri—2; Nebraska—3; South Carolina—1; Tennessee—1; Texas—4; Washington—1. The circumstances of the lynchings made plain the horror endured by black citizens with apparently scant preventive measures from federal or local authorities.

As never before in the history of America, black citizens responded to the attacks upon their race with an emotional outpouring of writings and speeches. The *Messenger* became the second journal (following the *Liberator*, edited by Max Eastman) to publish the poem "If We Must Die" by Claude McKay, a native of Jamaica who came to America to study and then remained to teach and write. During World War II, Winston Churchill used the powerful poem as part of the climax of his oration before the joint houses of the United States Congress.

Claude McKay wrote the lines as a defiant stance to lynching and mob attacks in Southern states:

> If we must die, let it not be like hogs
> Hunted and penned in an inglorious spot,
> While round us bark the mad and hungry dogs
> Making their mock at our accursed lot.
>
> If we must die, let it not be like hogs
> So that our precious blood will not be shed
> In vain; then even the monsters we defy
> Shall be constrained to honor us, though dead!
>
> O kinsmen! We must meet the common foe!
> Though far outnumbered, let us show us brave,
> And for their thousand blows deal one death-blow!
> What though before us lies the open grave?
>
> Like men we'll face the murderous, cowardly pack,
> Pressed to the wall, dying, but fighting back!

Countless black citizens felt the pain and disillusion evoked by "If We Must Die." The barriers separating the races were still high. Even DuBois, who had asked his race to "close ranks" shared his disillusionment in the May, 1919, issue of the *Crisis*, saying ". . . for America and her highest ideals we fought in far-off hope. . . . For America that represents and gloats in lynching, disenfranchisement, caste, brutality, and devilish insult—for this in its hateful upturning and mixing of things we were forced by vindictive fate to fight also. . . . We return—we return from fighting. We return fighting."

During this period of changes and challenges, the arrival of Marcus Garvey had altered the self-image of the poor and powerless in Harlem. Garvey was twenty-eight years old when he came to New York in March, 1916, from his homeland in Jamaica. An astute thinker and speaker, Garvey made a tour of the United States, studying the problems faced by the black race, especially the poor he described as "groping in the dark."

It was Randolph, courteous as always, who agreed to introduce Garvey at a Harlem street-corner meeting at 135th Street and Lenox Avenue. He later described that Garvey's powerful voice could be heard "from 135th to 125th Streets." James Weldon Johnson, who was then working as a columnist for *New York Age,* gave readers a vivid description of Garvey as "one of the most remarkable and picturesque figures that have appeared on the American scene."

In June, 1916, it was Hubert Harrison who introduced Garvey at a mass meeting held in Bethel A.M.E. Church with some two thousand attending. Johnson reported that Garvey "swept the audience along with him."

Within a short period, Garvey helped thousands of Harlem citizens see themselves in a new way. He quickly reasoned that the poor black, hard working people of Harlem had been left largely in the background and had been neglected in American society. Suddenly, the thousands in this group, many who migrated to Harlem and filled the jobs of European workers called to their native countries during the war, flocked to support Garvey, who called them beautiful and brilliant and gave them a place in the sun of publicity. The Garvey Movement was born.

Garvey's Universal Negro Improvement Association opened headquarters on 135th Street. Using his spell-binding speeches and a newspaper, *The Negro World*, Marcus Garvey motivated poor black people of Harlem to prize their unique beauty, their strength, their courage. He then preached to his followers to get organized.

Garvey's organization proved massive, colorful and spectacular. From across America, women who worked as domestics could dress as royalty in the spectacular Garvey parades. Men, regardless of their features or work or financial status, could also march regally.

Marcus Garvey constantly reminded followers of their history, giving them hope, saying, "You were once great; you shall be great again!"

Garvey's knowledge of crowd-pleasing psychology won followers from across the nation. His publication, *The Negro World*, included sections for Spanish and French-speaking readers. Liberty Hall, their meeting place, was huge enough to hold five or six thousand followers.

"We are striking homeward toward Africa to make her the big black republic," Garvey promised his followers. He gave them visions of retaking the 12,000,000 square miles of African territory that belonged to them by divine right.

Marcus Garvey became a world figure. His words and deeds were known by leaders around the world. With his "Back to Africa" ideas he persuaded followers to invest in the purchase of a fleet of ships, the "Black Star Line," that could transport black people to Africa where they could enjoy a new life. For further inspiration, Garvey declared himself "Provisional President of Africa."

As the Garvey movement increased in followers, Asa Randolph became disturbed. Although he admired the emphasis on racial pride, Randolph was concerned that Garvey's teachings would separate the black and white workers, while he had spent years trying to unite them in a common cause.

Suddenly Garvey's empire, which had been building for 10 years, collapsed, chiefly because of shady business dealings. He was also criticized for living in luxury while most of his followers were poor. Randolph joined the black leaders who spoke out in criticism of some of Garvey's methods. Randolph and his *Messenger* had begun to join other black leaders who gave the warning "Garvey must go!" The *Messenger* reported how in August, 1922, "more than two thousand people came out and listened to scholarly addresses upon the emptiness of Garvey's claims, the impossibilities of his schemes, the insincerity of the man."

The August 5, 1922, issue of Garvey's *Negro World* fired a response: "We say . . . to the Negro enemies of the past we are ready for you. . . . the Universal Improvement Association has no fears of anybody and when you interfere . . . you will take the consequences."

Garvey's empire collapsed when he was convicted of fraud in 1923. Sentenced to five years in an Atlanta penitentiary, he was pardoned by President Calvin Coolidge in 1927, but was deported to England. He died there, penniless, in 1940.

Meanwhile, holding to the belief that changes would come, Randolph turned his attention to helping black workers find suitable jobs. In 1920, Randolph and Owen organized the Friends of Negro Freedom, an interracial organization to help tenants and migrant workers find jobs and at the same time learn the benefits of socialism. Members of the Friends of Negro Freedom who lived in Harlem often came together on Sunday afternoons to discuss the problems of society. They seriously studied plans for helping black workers gain membership in unions. This effort failed, mainly because of discrimination.

By 1920, the *Messenger* became *The Only Radical Magazine Published by Negroes*. Later it became *A Journal of Scientific Ratification*, and in June, 1923, the editors declared it *The Opinion of the New Negro*. A year later this changed to *The World's Greatest Negro Monthly*. By then, advertising and contributions had diminished considerably.

Like the *Messenger*, the two editors floundered, trying to organize trade unions and help black workers who were still excluded from most of them. At least six of the political and trade unions they organized between 1917 and 1923 failed.

The one organization that lasted for a time was the Friends of Negro Freedom, organized in 1922. Guest lecturers to this intellectual forum included such notable speakers as Walter White of the NAACP; Will Durant, a historian; Algernon Lee of the Rand School of Social Science; and other well-known Americans.

The Friends of Negro Freedom became an organization Randolph thoroughly enjoyed. Many Sundays he invited the Friends to his apartment on West 142nd Street to have breakfast and discuss issues and politics. These distinguished guests seemed to enjoy these forums as much as Randolph. Two of the newcomers who especially admired Randolph were George Schuyler, a young editor new to Harlem, and Theophilus Lewis, the *Messenger*'s drama critic. Schuyler, who deeply admired Randolph, described the meetings of the Friends as "Athenian Conclaves" with Randolph presiding.

Randolph's brother, James, an intense scholar who in 1922 had come to live with his brother and attend City College, also thoroughly enjoyed the forum. Tall, handsome and a deep thinker like his brother, James had made plans to continue studies in Europe and eventually earn his doctorate.

A distinct honor came to Randolph and Owen in 1919 when Algernon Lee, who had become director of the Rand School of Social Science, invited them to join the school staff as part-time instructors.

Founded in 1916 by the American Socialists Society, the school was named for the abolitionist Carrie Rand, and offered instruction in courses on politics, literature and economics. Randolph and Owen provided lectures and guided discussions on "The Economics and Sociology of the Negro Program." Other faculty members of the Rand School included professors such as Charles A. Beard, Norman Thomas and Max Eastman. Beard, a noted American historian and political scientist, motivated Americans to take greater interest in their country's development through his teaching and publications on American history. Norman Thomas helped to found the American Civil Liberties Union (ACLU) and advocated many reforms that later became laws. Max Eastman wrote extensively about literature.

From the year 1917, Randolph and Owen realized with certainty that the future of black workers would depend upon alliances with trade unions. Randolph reasoned that the racial barriers that prohibited progress and promotions in trade unions should be eliminated.

The Friends of Negro Freedom, the most ambitious and lasting of the organizations, became the main feature for the *Messenger*'s May, 1922, issue. The goals of the interracial organization included the unionization of migrant workers, providing help to tenants and educating black people to understand the benefits of socialism.

In a storefront office on 131st Street, members of the Friends began spending hours discussing problems and laying plans for ways to unionize black workers. In time, the Friends became more of a social and intellectual forum.

Sad events clouded the years of 1922–24 for both Randolph and Owen. Toussaint, the brother of Owen and a master tailor, came from South Carolina hoping to find work in New York in 1922. After trying for several months, he became ill and died in March 1923.

The following year, at age sixty, Reverend James Randolph died in Jacksonville from a combination of heart and kidney ailments. Elizabeth Randolph moved to Harlem and lived with her two sons and Lucille.

In the October *Messenger*, Asa honored his father with a tribute "In Memorial to our Fallen Comrade:"

> Gentle in nature, broad in vision, philosophical in thinking, devoted to his family, his entire being ever devoted to the cause of Negro emancipation, the Reverend James Randolph passed into the unknown at his home in Jacksonville. . . . The death of such beautiful, rugged and stalwart, sacrificing characters is one of the tragedies of our period.

Still another change came when Chandler Owen left to take a position in Chicago where he worked as an editorial writer for the black newspaper the *Bee*. Owen continued to write for the *Messenger* and to elicit advertising space to publicize businesses. His name still appeared on the masthead of the journal as co-editor and his friendship with Randolph remained close.

Fortunately, Randolph also had the friendship of George Schuyler, whose brilliant editing and writing helped to keep the *Messenger* in print. The focus of the publication changed with the shifting events in America.

A major attraction in the 1920s was the publication of the works of young creative artists such as Countee Cullen, Langston Hughes and Claude McKay. Langston Hughes revealed that before he and his works had become well known, the *Messenger* bought his first short stories. Singers, including Roland Hayes and Paul Robeson, were also given publicity.

High praise for the *Messenger* also came from the *Call*, the periodical of the Socialist Party, citing the publication as "one of the most valuable and unique Socialist publications that has appeared in the country."

Eugene Debs, thoughtful as always, congratulated the *Messenger's* editors for "a splendid work in the education of your race and in the quickening of the consciousness of their class interests."

In 1921, another publication began to inspire black readers. Charles S. Johnson arrived from Chicago to become director of research for the New York office of the National Urban League, which was organized in 1911 as the "National League on Urban Conditions among Negroes." A voluntary community service agency, the League became dedicated to ending all discrimination based on creed or color. By January, 1923, Johnson had begun editing the magazine called *Opportunity: A Journal of Negro Life*. The name was derived from the Urban League's slogan, "Not alms, but opportunity."

In his search for fresh material from black writers, Johnson made public his belief that the most effective interest of the moment was art and then opened the pages to *Opportunity* for black writers and artists. He understood that a Renaissance was "powered by the mood of the blues" and made it possible for black writers and poets to feel free to publicize their creative efforts.

Encouraged by Johnson, Randolph and other black publishers also sought out black writers and artists to showcase their works. Citizens were encouraged to donate prizes and awards. Annual dinners were given at a downtown hotel where the prize winners were announced. Artists attending and receiving honors included Zora Neale Hurston, Langston Hughes, Claude McKay and Countee Cullen.

Musical background for these events was often provided by performers such as Cab Calloway and Duke Ellington; concert artists like Roland Hayes and Paul Robeson; and Broadway singers Florence Mills, Ethel Waters and Josephine Baker. More and more new black writers and artists were discovered and recognized.

Others also flourished. James Weldon Johnson, at that time a field secretary for the NAACP, published his *Book of American Negro Poetry*, two collections of Negro spirituals and a collection of Negro folk sermons in verse form entitled "God's Trombones." Johnson often spoke of his belief that art was a golden key to helping solve the race problem in the United States.

Alain Locke and other artists termed the Negro's sense of self and race a "spiritual emancipation." With this emancipation, old stereotypes began to be rejected and fewer attempts were made by black artists to imitate or conform to what was expected. This resulted in creativity in literature, the theater, music, dance. Broadway fell in love with jazz and the black artists who sang and played it—Ethel Waters, Bessie Smith, Duke Ellington, Jimmie Lunceford; dancers like Josephine Baker and "Bojangles" Robinson—all enjoyed creative freedom. Never before had America and the world showed such interest in the life and works of black citizens.

In time, the spirit of the Renaissance changed when commercialism took over. The black artists had no music companies, art galleries or concert halls. They could perform in many elegant nightclubs, but they were refused entrance otherwise because of racism. Nevertheless, the period had opened the door of opportunity in such a way that it could never be completely closed again.

Charles S. Johnson expressed pride in the strides of the Harlem Renaissance and the New Negro Movement: "Here was triumphantly the Negro artist, detached from propaganda, sensitive only to beauty."

The *Messenger* for May, 1923, illustrated in features and format how the publication had broadened in content and how its editors, like the nation, recognized the mounting influence and power of women in American life. The July, 1923, issue was dedicated to the "New Woman." This issue acknowledged in bold print on the cover: "New Negro Woman's Number," and the editorial column applauded "the New Negro Woman":

> Yes, she has arrived. . . . Upon her shoulders rests the big task to create and keep alive, in the breast of black men, a holy and consuming passion to break with the slave traditions of the past; to spurn and overcome the fugal, insidious inferiority complex of the present. . . . and to fight with increasing vigor, with dauntless courage, unrelenting zeal and intelligent vision of the stature of a full man for a free race and a new world.

America was changing. So was the world and black citizens, and also the *Messenger*. It announced the shifting focus from "A Journal of Scientific Radicalism" and in June, 1923, it became the "The New Opinion of the New Negro." After changing its focus several times, by 1924 contributions, advertisements and circulation had fallen. Randolph would later look back on this dilemma and tell friends, "It was a dark time for us. We were in the wilderness alone."

Randolph was still on a clear path to racial justice, however. In 1924, he helped to guide the black leaders and journalists who met with President Calvin Coolidge. The delegation requested that Coolidge grant a presidential pardon to some 70 black soldiers jailed for involvement in the 1917 riot in Houston, Texas, that was provoked by white attackers. A petition taken to the president by the delegation had been signed by 124,000 people, requesting that the imprisoned soldiers be released. As a result, many of the soldiers were eventually pardoned.

The *Messenger* heralded Randolph's response: "For once we presented a united front."

5

"FIGHT OR BE SLAVES"
1924–1925

> "You no longer have the wooden car, nor have you the typical porter. That porter has passed and a new porter has come into being. He is urbanized; he is industrialized, subject to this standardized civilization, and he is thinking through this new medium and it is organized labor."
>
> —A. Philip Randolph

The September, 1924, issue of the *Messenger* featured an article by Samuel Gompers, the powerful labor leader who in 1886 organized the American Federation of Labor (AFL) and served as the president and chief spokesman for that union until he died on December 13, 1924. True to his teachings, Gompers advocated economic objectives and encouraged workers to bargain for higher wages, but also for fewer working hours and better working conditions. He eventually built the AFL into the largest labor organization in the United States.

The *Messenger's* editor began to realize that his interest in labor reforms and unions had been noted by many Pullman porters, the men who served Pullman cars on railroad trains. Avid readers of the *Messenger*, many porters were known to hand out copies of the popular journal at train stops along their routes.

Each Pullman porter took pride in his neat appearance and in the courtesy and quality of his service to every passenger. (The Bettmann Archive)

The job as Pullman porter seemed one area in American labor in which black workers had exclusive domination. Randolph carefully reviewed their history, extending back to the emancipation of slaves in 1863, and including the assassination of President Abraham Lincoln on the evening of April 14, 1865.

By coincidence, George Mortimer Pullman had found a solution to the discomfort of long train rides across America that sometimes took several days. Born in Bracton, New York, on

George Mortimer Pullman (1831–97), American industrialist and inventor of the Pullman cars on railroad trains. (The Bettmann Archive)

March 3, 1831, Pullman was trained as a cabinet maker. In 1855, he moved to Chicago and began experimenting with the remodeling of old railroad coaches, determined to develop a "hotel on wheels." Finally, he succeeded and by 1864 had built his first luxurious car which gained immediate publicity when it was used to transport the body of President Abraham Lincoln from Chicago to Springfield, Illinois.

Over the next three years, Pullman developed and incorporated a leasing industry, the Pullman Palace Car Company, retaining ownership of the cars that he leased to various railroads. Passengers riding Pullman cars purchased special tickets and on a long-distance route, these riders remained in their Pullman cars, even if technically they changed trains several times.

Neatly attired, skillful Pullman porters were hired to help carry out Pullman's promise of a "palace on wheels." Readily available for hiring in late 1860s were hundreds of strong, healthy former slaves accustomed to laboring long hours without any salaries.

Pullman officials capitalized on the opportunity, setting strict guidelines for working and paying very low wages. Porters, therefore, depended upon tips from riders and worked hard to please the people they served. Even in the 1920s, a Pullman porter's salary was as low as $30.00 a month and from that he had to buy his own food and purchase items such as shoe polish and brushes to use in keeping garments of riders looking good. The primary job of Pullman porters was to keep the rich riders comfortable and happy throughout their long journey.

By 1915, Pullman was employing hundreds of black workers, more than any other company. Many of the young men were migrating from the South with aspirations of saving money and later attending college and becoming educated as certified professionals. Others were working to help support their families.

George Pullman reasoned that slaves accustomed to working daily for no salary would be adaptable to the long train rides with low pay. Also, former slaves were accustomed to being courteous and obedient, qualities which would satisfy Pullman riders. From the large labor force of former slaves, George Pullman hired porters for his parlor cars. For the porters, the opportunity to see different sections of the country and mingle with wealthy, learned citizens seemed a reasonable exchange for the long hours and service demanded by wealthy riders. The low wages paid kept the porters dependent upon tips and made them more anxious to please the riders.

Yet being a Pullman porter gave the men tremendous prestige. Many porters became outstanding leaders in churches, clubs and communities. Also, the constant mingling with learned, wealthy, talented riders served as learning trees, giving many porters diverse educational experiences.

From the outset, Pullman porters were trained to understand that their status as servants must be maintained, regardless of friendships formed with passengers during a long ride. Constant reminders reinforced the difference in status. For example, blankets for porters' beds were a different color from those of riders. Such symbolic segregation was used to remind porters that their status was inferior.

In addition to these reminders, porters also had to follow some blatantly exploitative regulations. One rule stipulated that porters had to purchase their uniforms and pay for all food they ate from the train's dining cars. They were also forced to use their own earnings to buy items needed to satisfy requests from riders.

Work schedule rules were grossly unfair as well. One rule, known as "running in charge," stipulated that a porter could be scheduled to carry on duties of a conductor, in addition to his own work, for an additional $12 a month. Regular conductors, all of them white, earned $120 a month.

Still another point for grievance was "doubling out," the practice of giving a porter orders to go out on a new run immediately after completing a long run, with no time to rest, and at a lower pay. Equally unfair was the ruling that an "extra porter" without a regular run might not get paid for work he performed on the train between noon and twelve midnight if the trip started at midnight.

Randolph's information-gathering included a review of labor leaders who pioneered for reform. High on his list was Eugene Victor Debs.

A believer in the organization of workers, Debs formed the American Railway Union (ARU) in 1893 and opened it to all railroad workers regardless of craft. In 1894, with support from Debs, the ARU members refused to move Pullman cars, showing support for workers who made the cars. Grover Cleveland, the United States president, ordered troops to break the strike, which, he charged, interfered with mail delivery. Eugene Debs was sent to prison for six months, charged with refusing to comply with a federal court injunction. By the time he left jail, he had become a confirmed supporter of socialism as a patriotic extension of America's democratic traditions.

Like Randolph, Debs was adamant in his criticism of the involvement of the United States in World War I. Arrested again while making a speech against the war, he was convicted under the Espionage Law and given a prison sentence of ten years.

While still in prison, Eugene Debs was nominated as a candidate for the presidency of the United States. Debs wrote of how he would "weep over the stark tragedy of the working class" as he worried about their poverty, misery, and despair. Prison officials permitted him to run his campaign from jail and to issue a press release each week. During the election, at least 919,000 ballots were cast for Convict 9653, as Eugene Debs was identified.

While in prison, Debs spent much of his time reading and writing about needed changes to help the inmates. In a booklet he titled "Walls and Bars," he outlined reforms needed in the prison systems. Whenever he had the attention of a listening group he often recited lines from his personal creed:

> While there is a lower class, I am in it.
> While there is a soul in prison, I am not free.

Constant public pressure from citizens who admired Debs influenced President Warren Harding to announce in December, 1921, that Debs was one of 24 prisoners who would have their sentences commuted. In freedom, weakened from his jailing, Debs still gave support to the Socialist Party. He also made clear his support of the Bolshevik Revolution, hoping that it would "become the beginning of self-government of the people throughout the world."

In a special letter, "For the *Messenger*," which was sent to Randolph from prison in Atlanta, Eugene Debs reminded the readership that:

> The historic mission of Socialism is to emancipate the workers of the world and the establishment of a system of society that is based on justice. The Socialist Party of America advocates the emancipation of the workers regardless of race, color, sex, or creed. . . . There cannot be a free nation of people when any part of the people are

Eugene V. Debs making an anti-war speech at Canton, Ohio, in 1918.
(UPI/Bettmann)

politically disfranchised or discriminated against. As long
as there is a master class that holds in subjugation wage
slaves there cannot be a free people.

Randolph later recalled when Eugene Debs graciously accepted an invitation to speak to a black audience. Debs emphasized his belief that blacks had as much potential for
development as whites, if given the chance. During his speech,
Debs praised Randolph's *Messenger* and underscored the importance of black people having their own press in order to
develop political power. Randolph remembered how attentive
the audience remained while Debs spoke. Over the years, his
speeches indicated a better understanding of hurdles which
blocked black citizens as they struggled to survive and to
succeed.

Sadly, Eugene Debs' eloquent voice was stilled when he
suffered a massive heart attack on October 15, 1926. He died
five days later.

By that time, Asa Randolph had decided that his life, like that of Debs, would become intertwined with the future of workers and unions. His decision became firm after he studied the problems faced by one of the best known groups of black workers in America.

The turn of events began on a June morning in 1925 as Randolph took his usual brisk walk to the *Messenger's* office. Along the way, a well-attired man stopped him and introduced himself as Ashley L. Totten, a Pullman sleeping car porter. On his way to Randolph's office, Totten added that he had heard Randolph speak during a soapbox session and knew of his interest in motivating workers to organize.

That day, Ashley Totten shared with Randolph the chief concerns of the Pullman porters, and their need for a union that could bargain for improved wages and working conditions. Porters were governed by the company's "Plan of Employee Representation" which was controlled by Pullman officials. The porters had decided to organize their own union and, knowing of Randolph's urging for workers to bargain from strength, they needed his leadership.

The one person who could best help them, porters had decided, was Asa Randolph. He had interest and experience in organizing black workers, and the porters respected his logic and dedication as a fearless crusader for justice and equality for all citizens. The porters also knew of Randolph's reputation that he could not be "bought or sold" regardless of enticements. Furthermore, Randolph was independent, not under the domination of any boss who might attempt to restrict his words or control his actions.

Interested, but having experienced the roadblocks of trying to organize a union of black workers, Randolph asked for time to study the possibilities. He knew the problems faced by workers of his race, excluded from membership in unions, and, therefore, denied the pay and privileges established under bargained agreements.

When Randolph addressed small groups of porters, they were so impressed by his command of words that a few of them planned a secret meeting in the home of a well-established porter, W. H. DesVerney. The group agreed upon a mission for Randolph. Would he be willing to speak to a group of porters on procedures for organizing a union of workers?

Randolph was kept busy trying to keep the *Messenger* in print but he promised to consider the idea. His consideration included a review of the history of Pullman porters which made clearer their need for help in forming an organized group.

In earlier years, Pullman porters were considered an elitist group of workers, photographed in their neat uniforms, with pleasant smiles on their faces while they catered to white riders. These photos gave the public the impression that all porters were happy and pleased with their jobs and content with their working conditions. Their positions were envied because they worked in a luxurious environment, mingling with wealthy and famous riders. During the decades following slavery, early porters accustomed to no pay for hard labor were gratified for the low salary and whatever tips they received. By the 1920s, however, the expectations of porters had expanded with their experiences. Some of them had been educated in high schools and even colleges. The majority held key positions in their communities. They traveled to distant places, mingled with wealthy passengers and read widely during the long train rides. Porters were no longer "Pullman's slaves" or "wage slaves" as they were once known, and they wanted to be treated like citizens, not as servants.

One of the most frustrating factors for porters was the ruling that regardless of the quality or the responsibilities of their work, job classifications remained the same. The job as porter was as high as they could hope to attain. There was no promotional rung to climb. These black workers were destined to remain in the role originally cast for them in the 1860s—grateful servants, always smiling, never complaining, ever ready to help—but always obedient to superiors.

By the 1920s, the Pullman porters, like most American labor groups, made salaries and benefits major issues in negotiations. The Pullman Company had developed into one of America's industrial giants. The Pullman porters had made equally remarkable progress. Many were homeowners, highly respected citizens, and leaders in their communities. Children of porters were attending colleges.

With this progress and elevation in citizenship and experience, Pullman porters began requesting pay on a scale nearer to that of other workers performing comparable jobs. In response, Pullman officials argued that the wages of porters were supplemented by tips from satisfied Pullman passengers.

There were other grievances. The Pullman porters were required to report for work several hours before departure of their train in order to prepare for passengers and then help them board the train. The porters' time for payment, however, began when the train departed the station.

Passing years brought revolutionary changes to Pullman porters and to railroad trains. During miles of train rides, the usual barriers of race and class were often forgotten while wealthy passengers and porters exchanged friendships, each learning from the other in diverse ways, though by company policy, this was not condoned.

Each generation of porters became better educated. Nevertheless, continuing racism restricted job opportunities as well as income. Even with college training, some porters preferred to remain a "travelin' man" rather than move on to professional jobs available to them. Now, with Randolph's leadership, they hoped to challenge the outmoded barriers constructed by racial prejudice and antiquated practices. Pullman porters were no longer content to remain Pullman slaves.

Asa Randolph's varied experiences seemed to have been preparing him for leadership in this historic undertaking. With confidence in this mission, he called together a committee of porters who helped him plan a meeting to organize their new union, which, like many working groups in America, they envisioned as a "Brotherhood"—the Brotherhood of Sleeping Car Porters. For American workers, the term Brotherhood evoked the sense of togetherness, a banding together for a common cause.

On the evening of August 25, 1925, the Brotherhood of Sleeping Car Porters met in the auditorium of the Imperial Lodge of Elks on West 129th Street, with about 500 porters in attendance. Present also were several porters spotted as spies, listening to take information back to Pullman officials.

Conscious of this danger, Randolph told the porters he would run the meeting himself, and he did, from the singing of the Brotherhood song, "Hold the Fort," to making announcements and introductions of guest speakers and then giving the main address. He told the porters what the Brotherhood would be demanding from the Pullman Company: recognition of the union, an end to tipping, a monthly wage of $150, compensation for extra work and the payment of a conductor's wage when performing a conductor's work.

The porters listened intently and followed directions. Randolph cited specific changes that the Brotherhood would demand, specifically recognition of the new union as the bargaining agent. Furthermore, Randolph demanded that porters be treated as men.

The Brotherhood of Sleeping Car Porters had become a reality. The *Messenger's* office began to double as the office of the Brotherhood, and on the first day after the meeting over 200 porters came to join the new union.

Their leader boldly planned the next steps. He decided that Brotherhood offices had to be established in Pullman terminals all across the country. A mammoth membership drive needed to be organized. For this, a treasury had to be established.

With the daring of pioneering men like his father, Asa Randolph planned his next steps. Each would require money.

Help came from a Jacksonville native. James Weldon Johnson had been chosen a member of the board of 12 directors charged with distributing a large sum of money inherited and then donated by Charles Garland, a wealthy American who wanted his inheritance of millions distributed, with instructions that the funds be given away "as quickly as possible," and "*without regard to race, creed, or color.*" At Johnson's suggestion, a grant of ten thousand dollars from the Garland Fund enabled the Brotherhood to establish offices in major American cities with Pullman terminals.

Asa Randolph then began a series of whirlwind trips to assist the Brotherhood leaders of major terminals in organizing offices and in convincing all porters of the values of joining unions.

6

"A GOOD MAN AT THE TOP"
1926–1927

"Brethren . . . when I enlisted in the cause, I knew . . . that I would be branded as a disturber of the peace, as a madman, fanatic, an incendiary, a Communist, anarchist, and whatnot. . . . knew that the base and servile would accuse me of being actuated by the hope of reward. But, Brethren, I am undaunted and unafraid. . . . Let us not hate our detractors, for they must be saved with the expansive and redeeming love of the Brotherhood."

—A. Philip Randolph

The new legend on the masthead of the periodical proclaimed the dramatic changes taking place: the *Messenger* had become "The Official Organ of the Brotherhood of Sleeping Car Porters." As editor, Randolph realized the significance of a "Brotherhood" to men of his race and set a goal to organize a union of black workers that the world would in time feel compelled to respect.

The hard-working, poorly paid porters sensed the compassion and vision of their leader and began paying the membership dues of $3 each month. Some porters came to Randolph's office and brought their money. Other porters, afraid of being reported to Pullman officials, secretly sent their monthly payment to the Brotherhood.

Randolph knew that in order to forge a unified group of workers, porters all across the United States should be organized. He was then close to being penniless. Yet, he knew the importance of making personal contacts with the porters to learn their problems. And, he wanted to inspire them with the hope of a strong Brotherhood in future years. Unable to help them financially himself, Randolph used part of the grant from the Garland Fund.

By October, Randolph was ready to begin a national organizational tour that he hoped would include meetings in most of the major Pullman terminals, assisting porters and helping them to gain strength by maintaining a unified Brotherhood. He planned the first stop for Chicago. Before he arrived, he had been advised that the porter to see in Chicago was Milton Webster.

A Tennessee native, Webster, at age thirty-eight, was tall, with a powerful body, stern countenance and a heavy, gruff voice. He had worked as a Pullman porter for 20 years until he was fired for trying to organize a union. Webster agreed to interest a group of porters in attending a series of organizational meetings to be held nightly for two weeks.

Porters in attendance recalled the rapt attention when Randolph began speaking and reported that "you could hear a pin drop." He gave the porters vision of a new Brotherhood when they would be earning more than double their present pay because they would have their own union.

By the time Randolph finished speaking, Webster was voicing his approval. However, Webster and other porters were disappointed that many black officials invited to the meetings to speak to the porters failed to attend. As Webster recalled, the nightly meetings had two speakers, "Me opening and Brother Randolph closing."

A later session brought unexpected excitement. Perry Howard, a black Republican national committeeman and a special assistant to the United States Attorney General, challenged Randolph to engage in a debate with him. Randolph graciously accepted the challenge. The topic chosen for debate concerned the "right and necessity and value" of the Pullman porters organizing a union.

Later, Webster gleefully gave the results: "Howard showed up all right, in the biggest hall in the Negro section. In almost less time that it takes to tell, Randolph had run him out of gas. I got my coat ripped off helping the police get Howard out."

Randolph's calm, assured manner during the debate influenced many porters in the packed auditorium. The Chicago division of the Brotherhood suddenly expanded with new members.

Ashley Totten had arrived in time to listen to the debate. His request for permission to stop over in Chicago had been denied by Pullman officials who knew his reason for the visit. When Totten stopped over anyway, he was immediately fired on charges of "unsatisfactory services."

During the next evening's meeting, immediately after Webster's opening remarks, Ashley Totten jumped to the platform, and began addressing the audience. In Webster's words, he "strutted his stuff." Totten, like many other Pullman employees, was ready to work for revolutionary changes.

Webster surmised this and reportedly whispered advice to Randolph: "Take that man along with you."

Randolph accepted the advice. By the time the Chicago sessions ended, the two men had established a close friendship. Both were independent and strong-willed, but both were deeply committed to the building of a strong Brotherhood. Randolph appointed Webster organizer of the Chicago division, and also general manager of the national movement to organize the Brotherhood. Chandler Owen, who worked as an editorial writer for the *Chicago Bee*, accepted membership on the organizing committee.

With headquarters for the Chicago division of the Brotherhood temporarily established in the Metropolitan Community Church, and with Webster in control, Randolph continued his travels to establish Brotherhood offices and leaders. Totten now traveled with him. In each city visited, they met strong, unique personalities, all committed to forming a strong Brotherhood.

In St. Louis they met E. J. Bradley, a man with large, deep-set eyes who had worked for 30 years as a Pullman porter, but let Randolph know that he would not retire because "nobody can organize St. Louis but me." He was needed. When Pullman officials learned that porters had been visiting the office that Bradley set up, the porters were all fired. Eventually forced to give up his secretary, then his office space in a bank building, Bradley set up a makeshift office in the trunk of his car and continued recruiting Brotherhood members.

Other porters faced similar hardships and firings. In Oakland there was a retired porter named Morris Moore, affectionately known as "Dad Moore." People remarked that he reminded them of India's Mahatma Gandhi. Dad Moore's job in retirement was taking care of old sleeping cars and making them comfortable places where porters could stay during layovers. Dad would wake the porters in time to board their connecting trains. Randolph became Dad Moore's idol and, during his visit in Oakland, Moore followed him wherever he walked. He began working for Randolph and the Brotherhood, knowing the Pullman policy that under their rules, his pension would be terminated if he engaged in any union activity.

From city to city, Randolph kept moving, organizing and inspiring porters. The trips were grueling and the traveling accommodations, for all black travelers, were uncomfortable and wearisome. Wherever he visited porters, Randolph encouraged them with hope for changes. He continued to win new members for their union. The porters began to realize that Randolph inspired as much as he taught and many treasured the inspiration given them.

Many of these porters inspired by Randolph later became leaders of the great civil rights movement that revolutionized race relations in America and in the world. E. D. Nixon of Birmingham, Alabama, often recalled in speeches and in his autobiography how Randolph inspired him with his command of thoughts and words. "When I heard Randolph speak, it was like a light," Nixon said. "I was determined that I was gonna fight for freedom until I was able to get some of it myself."

Most American citizens later knew Nixon for his courage as he, along with Rosa Parks, Dr. Martin Luther King, Jr., and other brave black leaders in Montgomery, Alabama, organized the boycott of public buses, and added the fuel that ignited the civil rights movement of the 1960s.

Working tirelessly, Randolph established Brotherhood offices in one major city after another. Despite the long, exhausting trips and meetings after meetings, he refused to take time for a vacation or even to relax. The porters would have their union, he promised. With a union, they could begin to negotiate for reform. Realizing that many black workers, denied membership in trade unions, did not fully realize the difference between company unions and trade unions, Randolph took

Officers of the Brotherhood of Sleeping Car Porters in the 1930s. (Chicago Historical Society)

time to explain why it was important for black workers to continue battling against bars that kept racial groups excluded, reducing chances for promotions and benefits.

Wherever Randolph spoke, porters and other black workers listened in fascination. Randolph's gentle, yet always elegant speech and manners held a charm for porters who had been viewed by their bosses as servants, a slight step above slaves. The porters began to revere Randolph. To many, he became "The Chief," strong and daring to give courage and inspire porters to battle one of the wealthiest companies in the world.

An astute observer, Randolph noted that many of the Pullman porters had become leaders in their churches, in civic organizations and in the overall advancement of community life. When he visited a Brotherhood group as speaker, he began to use terms that evoked among the listeners familiar and reassuring phrases and thoughts. Whenever possible, the meetings were held in churches. Despite the fact that Randolph professed to be an atheist, his gentle ways, compassionate understanding and unselfish giving reflected for many people who knew him the qualities needed for leadership as taught in the Bible. His meetings with a gathering of porters would usually begin with prayers and the Brotherhood members understood that their Chief illustrated the teachings of Christianity, devoting his life and his talents to bring about reforms, not for himself, but for all Americans.

The strong, pioneering porters Randolph chose as Brotherhood organizers adopted their Chief's unselfish type of leadership, which in turn was reflected by the porters under their supervision. The group of earlier organizing supervisors included, along with "Dad" Moore and C. L. Dellums of Oakland, California, E. J. Bradley of St. Louis, Missouri, and Benjamin Smith of Omaha, Nebraska. They, as well as other Brotherhood branch leaders, knew that their position made them targets for intimidation from powerful Pullman forces. Like their Chief, each of the bold organizers had the vision and toughness that enabled them to look toward future progress, not present fear of punishment.

Fortunately, Randolph was able to secure the services of Frank Crosswaith, a prominent labor organizer, who assisted him in the New York office and handled affairs during the periods when Randolph traveled to assist and motivate porters as they established Brotherhood offices. Accustomed to the dehumanizing attitude of many white bosses, the porters developed high respect for Randolph's inspiring talks with them, his obvious interest in their welfare and, above all, his assurance that the future for black workers would erase many of the present-day problems and conflicts.

The Brotherhood members adopted the optimistic vision of their leader. They began to plan for the future with confidence.

7

THE STRUGGLES FOR JUSTICE
1926–1927

"The Brotherhood is showing black men
and women, and Pullman officials, that
money is not everything, and that the
spirit and the will of the people for justice
is unconquerable."

—A. Philip Randolph

Randolph kept on the move, winning the confidence of porters and enlarging membership in the Brotherhood union. With the help of dedicated porters, he was able to establish Brotherhood organizations in major American cities from coast to coast.

The constant traveling was both expensive and exhausting but he knew the value of meeting the Pullman porters face to face, listening to their grievances and sharing their problems. Realizing the abuse and racial discrimination that many of the porters endured from Pullman bosses and passengers, he was determined to find solutions for problems and concerns.

As he talked with porters, Randolph understood why many of them were hesitant to join the Brotherhood union. They were afraid of being fired as soon as their membership was discovered by Pullman officials. Another reason was lack of money. The meager salary earned by porters was barely enough to support their families.

In every state visited, Randolph met loyal porters who could be classified as heroes. Benjamin (Bennie) Smith, a tall porter with military bearing, was one of them. A close friend of Milton Webster, Smith worked for the Pullman Company, but doubled as a spy for the Brotherhood, feeding reports to Randolph or

Webster and keeping them abreast of plans. Pullman eventually fired Smith, and Randolph immediately hired him to help Ashley Totten organize a Brotherhood division in Kansas City, Missouri.

Smith's boldness and skills inspired Randolph to send him to open an office in Jacksonville, Florida. If successful, it would be the first Brotherhood division in a state of the South. Knowing the racism he might encounter, Smith pretended to be a *Messenger* salesman. In this role, he was soon arrested on charges of preaching social equality in the South and threatened to be "taken to a tree."

Smith realized that this warning meant he would be lynched. He wired his dilemma to Randolph who ordered him to leave Jacksonville at once. Milton Webster's advice to Smith was more forceful: "Get the hell out of Jacksonville. You can't beat no case down there." Barely escaping death, Smith left immediately. He later successfully organized a Brotherhood division in Detroit, Michigan.

States of the South were not alone in their stand against Randolph and the Brotherhood. The Pullman Company also counted upon support from the black community, especially from some of the churches and newspapers that were black owned and edited. On the other hand, many New York churches and their ministers did give strong support to the Brotherhood, including Adam Clayton Powell, Sr., and the Abyssinian Baptist Church; Reverend Lloyd Imes and St. James Presbyterian Church; and the Reverend Frederick Cullen and Salem Methodist Church.

Several churches invited the porters to hold meetings in their facilities. When the information circulated that Randolph had refused offers of large sums of money if he would end his determination to organize the porters, support for the Brotherhood became stronger among porters who were hesitant initially. Also, as the nation's economic condition slowed, many citizens began to feel the pinch. As the financial downturn in America's economy continued, more citizens began to realize the unselfishness of Randolph and the Brotherhood leaders who sometimes worked for partial pay or for no salary at all.

Eventually, closer cooperation between black churches and the Brotherhood of porters enabled the church members and Pullman porters to maintain a cooperative alliance, each offering unified support to the other. Randolph revised some of the harsh criticisms of churches he had made in earlier times. He realized that many of the Brotherhood members were church leaders who could influence churchgoers and win their confidence and support. A struggling Brotherhood of black porters needed both.

Randolph's voice carried out the mission in his way. His powerful speech reached his race in a mission that became more important to him and to the nation. His resonant voice touched and motivated church crowds in a manner he might never have mastered as an entertainer, or even as a minister.

In meetings to shore up morale of porters, the Brotherhood Chief often selected verses from the Biblical storehouse his father had used to inspire church attendants during the days of Florida's development, when many people scoffed at the idea that the state might one day attract citizens from all over the United States and the world. Randolph, like his father, frequently used Biblical words and phrases in his speeches, closing with lines such as: "Stand upon thy feet and the God of Truth and Justice and Victory will speak to thee."

Morale was not the only element of the Brotherhood that needed strengthening. Legal fees, including payment to several advisors, took a heavy toll on the Brotherhood treasury. Randolph kept the porters informed on procedures and the eventual benefits he hoped to gain for them. On October 15, 1926, after several attempts to establish communication with the Pullman Company and its president, E. G. Carry, Randolph notified the Board of Mediation of the dispute between the Brotherhood and the Pullman Company. The Mediation Board then assigned Edward P. Morrow, a former governor of Kentucky, to investigate the disputes. A preliminary inquiry was scheduled for December, 1926. For the Brotherhood, Randolph hired Donald P. Richburg, an expert in labor laws. Answering to an appeal, porters contributed what funds they could toward the legal fees.

At the preliminary inquiry held by Morrow, the Brotherhood reported a membership that numbered more than half of the porters. However, the Pullman officials' report showed that by their count, 85 percent of the porters had voted for representation by the Pullman Company's Plan of Employee Representation. According to these figures, then, the Brotherhood would not have a majority representation and therefore could not act on the porters' behalf.

On the basis of this report, Morrow adjourned the inquiry until further instruction was issued.

Surprised and disappointed, Randolph understood that many porters, fearful of being fired, had been frightened into voting for the Company union, even though they had stated their preference for the Brotherhood. But Randolph, well schooled in labor law, also understood that any coercion by either side would violate the rules of the Railway Labor Act.

Randolph began to gather evidence regarding the Pullman figures from the porters. At least 900 of them stated under oath that Pullman officials had forced them to vote as they did. Then the long wait began for the final report. Meanwhile, as Webster wrote to Randolph from Chicago, porters were becoming uneasy. Many of them had become frightened and stopped paying Brotherhood dues.

Knowing what they were up against, Randolph kept insisting that the Brotherhood would surely win in the end. Throughout the procedures, Randolph counted on the core of staunch members, those he called the "pure gold of the Brotherhood."

Randolph also continued to display an outward calm and confidence. He realized that more than ever the Pullman porters looked to him for guidance and inspiration to maintain their confidence in his leadership. The porters needed their Chief's uplifting approach to problems. They needed to know that their struggles were worthwhile and that their fight had just begun.

8

YEARS OF CHANGE AND CHALLENGE 1928–1934

> "Salvation for a race, nation, or class must come from within. Freedom is never granted; it is won. Justice is never given; it is exacted."
>
> —A. Philip Randolph

Though uneasiness and fear continued to shake much of the Brotherhood, the porters continued to support Randolph's leadership abilities. However, membership in the Brotherhood continued to decline because of firings within the Pullman Company and because of worsening economic conditions. Seeing that conditions were not improving, Randolph decided to take his case to the president of the United States.

Along with a group of black leaders, Randolph met with President Calvin Coolidge in January, 1928. In a style practiced by Coolidge, he sat silent while Randolph explained the problems facing the Pullman porters, nodding his head to indicate understanding of Randolph's explanation of such problems as the low wages and the intolerable working conditions.

Randolph explained a strike possibility, informing Coolidge that "because you may be in the position of having to take action at that time, I wanted to let you know what the facts are, and what my union is trying to accomplish." When the meeting ended, President Coolidge thanked Randolph for his visit, smiled and the two men shook hands. Nothing concrete seemed to have been accomplished.

The next step for Randolph was a meeting in New York with officers of the Brotherhood to bring them up-to-date on the events. He did not know what Coolidge would do, he told them, but he was ready to go ahead and call a strike vote. It was, perhaps, their only chance to force the Company to talk with them.

This was a crucial decision for Brotherhood members. A strike could mean weeks, perhaps months, without pay. The young union had no treasury of strike funds. Also, the nation's economy showed signs of weakness. People were losing jobs. These jobless workers could easily replace the porters if they went on strike.

Understanding their fears, Randolph explained the significance of the strike vote and how it was used. The vote for a strike did not necessarily mean a strike would take place, but it did give union leaders the right to call a strike. A strike vote was often used to force a company to begin bargaining with workers.

Randolph seemed confident as the porters voted in April, 1928. More than 6,000 porters voted in favor of the strike, with only 17 members voting against it. The date for beginning the strike was set for June 8, and Randolph explained that if by then the Company still refused to bargain with them, every Pullman porter in the country would walk off the job and the trains would not run. People would realize, he added, that they represented a new Pullman porter and the spirit of the New Negro.

By law, the next decision was up to the Mediation Board. Before the time set for the strike to begin, the Board announced a decision: No emergency exists. A strike by Pullman porters would not cause a transportation crisis. Therefore, the Mediation Board made no recommendation to the president.

Stunned, Randolph went immediately to Washington to meet with members of the Mediation Board. How could they rule this way? he questioned.

The Mediation Board members gave no satisfactory explanation. It became clear to Randolph, however, that the Board was protecting the Pullman Company, the employer, and not the porters, the employees. That fight was a failure, with the odds all in favor of the Pullman Company.

Randolph also met with William Green, the current president of the American Federation of Labor (AFL). Green had shown constant sympathy for the Brotherhood and Randolph could rely on him for sound advice. Furthermore, if the porters did eventually strike, they would need support from Green and the AFL members.

Green listened with understanding as Randolph reviewed the struggle of the porters over the past months. He learned that the Pullman Company had already targeted a group of workers to take over the jobs of porters who went on strike. Additional police had also been alerted so that they could move into the rail terminals and control actions the minute a strike started.

Green asked about the porters and whether they would walk off the job if the Brotherhood called a strike. Randolph responded with an honest answer. He did not really know. Most of the porters were poor and they were afraid of losing their jobs even if the working conditions were unfair.

The two labor leaders weighed the advantages and disadvantages for both sides of the dispute. Green finally gave a blunt analysis: A strike would fail. Green reminded Randolph that many workers were out of jobs and might willingly replace striking porters. Sadly, but honestly, Randolph was forced to agree.

The Brotherhood Chief was not about to surrender, however. Randolph forwarded an open letter to all porters and maids, promising them that the strike was "merely postponed" and giving them confidence with his familiar challenge: "The fight has just begun." There was one last chance of victory. The Railway Labor Act stipulated that in the occurrence of any interruption to commerce or the operation of any carrier, the powers of the Mediation Board could again be invoked.

Randolph interpreted this to mean that the union could call a strike. It would, thereby, create an emergency.

The Brotherhood decided to create an "emergency" by calling for a strike vote, thereby showing the ability and readiness of the Brotherhood union to call a strike against the Pullman Company.

The porters responded. Of the 10,999 porters, 6,013 voted to walk off the Pullman cars as soon as the strike order was issued.

Assured, the Brotherhood officials went back to the Mediation Board, stating that its strike vote indicated that an emergency would be created in the Pullman service, and asking that an emergency board be established to resolve the crisis.

Edward P. Morrow, chief investigator for the Mediation Board, summoned Randolph and heard his side of the dispute, but by then, a decision in the matter had been reached. Pullman Company officials assured Morrow that the Brotherhood would not be capable of disrupting Pullman car services. Furthermore, since the Pullman Company would suffer most from an emergency, the Company, not the union, should inform the Mediation Board if an emergency existed.

Again, as in the first attempt at mediation, a letter arrived from the Mediation Board to inform Randolph that "it is the judgment of our Board that at this time an emergency . . . does not exist in this case."

In the end, the power and influence of the wealthy Pullman outfit won. In July, the Mediation Board "retired" the case. Once again, Randolph had failed to win, and felt that he had let the porters down. To him, the disappointment was "next to the saddest moment" of his life. The saddest had been the unexpected death of his brother James, at age forty-one, in January 1928, during a devastating epidemic of diphtheria.

James had outlined future plans for studying languages and mathematics at the University of Berlin. During his stay in Harlem, he had won friends and admirers with his brilliant thinking and likeable personality.

"I can't bear to live in a world without my brother," Randolph confided to a friend. Nevertheless, he masked his grief and continued his fight for the Pullman porters, determined to "put the Brotherhood on top."

The 1929 stock market collapse and the Great Depression that followed conditioned the course of Randolph's planning. Black Americans in both rural and urban settings felt the force of the impact. Banks closed their doors and millions of people lost their savings. Businesses shut down. The jobless and the homeless multiplied as the Great Depression worsened. Within a few months, at least 300,000 workers were without jobs.

Customarily, African-American workers were the last hired and became the first to lose jobs. Worse, the laborious and dirty work once refused by other ethnic groups became acceptable when the alternative was starvation and homelessness. Even the Brotherhood could no longer count upon the historic traditions that all Pullman porters hired would be African Americans.

Asa Randolph traveled from one city to another, motivating Pullman porters to keep faith in their country and in their Brotherhood. Despite the economic jolt of the Depression years, he never lost faith that porters would have an independent union. As their Chief, he gave the workers inspiration with his optimistic outlook, motivating them to face the future with hope.

As more and more Pullman porters lost jobs, the Brotherhood treasury dwindled. Randolph refused a salary but continued working to win the recognition and power granted to independent labor unions.

Porters took pride in boasting about their new-style leader, their Chief. Traditionally, leaders operated apart from the masses, handing down decisions and directions. Randolph acted as a member of the masses. He believed in sharing ideas as opposed to handing down commands. The Pullman porters recognized this and gained strength from Randolph's unselfishness. In turn, the dogged determination by Brotherhood members to build and maintain a first-rate union motivated Randolph to give the porters and the entire black race at least a propelling start toward revolutionary racial advancement.

As the Great Depression deepened, porters were losing jobs and needed money for their families. Recollections of these Depression days documented the determination of porters to follow Randolph's example and sacrifice so that they could make the nation's first all-black union a successful reality.

The porters gained inspiration from the unselfish leadership of their Chief. Friends close to Randolph began to notice the difference in his physical appearance as the battle with Pullman forces continued and the economic downturn persisted. Known for his fashionable, immaculate grooming, his time-worn suits showed the shine of constant wear. His economic status had obviously changed as the disastrous depression affected Lucille's thriving beauty business. Most black women could no longer afford such luxuries as hair treatments and manicures. Like countless American families, the Randolphs suddenly had very little money to spend. Lucille could no longer afford fashionable new clothes. Randolph wore his favorite blue serge suit over and over. Porters noted that his shoes showed holes in the bottom.

As the depression continued, hope for Randolph and the Brotherhood turned to gloom. More and more porters lost homes because they lost jobs and could not pay mortgages or rent. Without money for dues, membership in the Brotherhood continued to dwindle. Most of the offices were forced to close. The New York office was later seized for nonpayment of the mortgage; its contents, including furniture and precious papers, were scattered in the streets.

Despite the setbacks, Randolph insisted that the Brotherhood operate as a first-rate organization. His correspondence was usually printed on elegant stationery. He insisted that speeches given by Brotherhood leaders should have uplifting themes. Everything about their organization, he believed, should remain classy and inspire the workers.

Many porters adopted this belief. They loved their Chief and knew he was devoting his life to help them. When some porters learned that Randolph was reduced to one good shirt, they sacrificed money set aside for their own needs and bought him two fashionable shirts. The soles of his shoes showed evidence of the miles he had walked. Still, the Chief's head was high, his carriage regal, his words always inspirational.

In later years, porters would share stories of these hard times. None of them had known with certainty how they would survive the Great Depression. Ashley Totten recalled how on Christmas Eve he did not even have enough money for carfare to get home to his wife and children in Queens. Along with another porter in similar straits, he spent Christmas Eve in the Brotherhood office, using his coat for covering and newspapers for a mattress. Totten told how he broke down and cried—something he had not done since childhood.

Other Brotherhood members shared similar accounts of hardships. They began to form networks of creative money-making activities to help families of porters in critical straits. Some porters even volunteered to work extra shifts and used the money to assist those who had been fired and faced such crises as losing homes or removing children from college.

In a popular money-making project known as the "rent parties," porters would take turns in giving parties to help themselves, or other Brotherhood members. They raised money to pay for rent, house mortgages, loans and for other essential needs.

Wives of porters organized money-making projects and formed networks to collect food for families of porters who were destitute. Lucille Randolph spearheaded the planning of many of these fund-raising efforts despite the financial setbacks she faced. As more and more customers could no longer afford the luxury of a beauty salon, her business dipped financially lower and lower.

The Depression still persisted even though Herbert Clark Hoover, the thirty-first United States President (1929–33), encouraged citizens that times would get better.

Change came in 1932 when the presidential election was won by Franklin Delano Roosevelt, who immediately began establishing innovative laws and economic programs that resulted in working people having greater power and economic strength. As the former New York governor, Franklin Roosevelt was known for his support of workers and for the projects and new programs that provided training and jobs for all racial groups. Gradually, the Depression began to ebb.

As expected, Randolph sought help for the porters, hoping to benefit from the protection of new laws that affected railroads. With the help of his friend, William Green, and a convincing appearance before Congress, Randolph succeeded. The Railway Labor Act was amended, giving employees "the right to organize and bargain collectively through representatives of their own choosing . . . free from the interference, restraint, or coercion of employers of labor, or their agents." This change gave the Pullman porters legal rights to form a union of their own. Further, their employer would be compelled to recognize their union.

The goal of the Brotherhood seemed at last within reach. Randolph forwarded a letter to officials of the Pullman Company, requesting a meeting. The company's response was curt, citing that there was no occasion for a meeting. The letter repeated the company's insistence that the Brotherhood did not represent the Pullman porters.

Now confident, Randolph sought clarification from the Mediation Board in Washington. This time, the Board ordered that an election be held to determine which organization would represent Pullman porters.

The official voting took place in cities and towns across the United States. The final tally showed at least 8,316 votes for the Brotherhood, and 1,422 for the Company's Pullman's Protective Association.

Randolph's 10-year struggle to gain recognition for the Brotherhood had been worth the efforts. The significance of the victory was shared by Randolph with Walter White of the NAACP. The election, Randolph said, would mark a historic point in the efforts of the Negro workers in the trade union movement. He viewed the porters as the vanguard of the black workers in America.

A telegram from the Urban League phrased congratulations in two brief sentences: "No labor leadership in America has faced greater odds. None has won a greater victory."

The moment of truth came on a late July day of 1935. Asa Randolph led a small group of Brotherhood officials into a conference room of the Pullman Building in Chicago. The Pullman Company president, A. J. Curry, did what he had vowed he would never do. He sat at the same table with leaders he had described as a "bunch of black porters."

One of those porters, C. L. Dellums, recalled the drama of participating. None of the porters had special training in negotiations. "But here we were," Dellums said, "around this wonderful man [Randolph]."

On August 25, 1937, Randolph remained calm and confident as usual as Curry not only sat, but negotiated and signed the agreement with the Brotherhood. The contract assured that the Brotherhood would be the official union to speak for the porters. For the first time in American history, a union of black workers signed a contract with a prominent American company. Under the contract, the long traveling hours of the porters were lessened from eleven thousand miles a month to seven thousand miles. A new wage agreement added nearly $2 million dollars in extra pay.

Asa Randolph was cheered by members of his race as their most popular leader of the era. The Brotherhood's victory became cause for celebration by black Americans across the United States. That August 25 was the birthday of the new Brotherhood of Sleeping Car Porters.

The Brotherhood had become the first union of black workers to be awarded an international charter in the fifty-seven year history of the American Federation of Labor. Families and friends of porters planned special celebrations. Some communities celebrated with picnics and dinners. Churches held prayer meetings to give thanks. Even African Americans in faraway places marked the event with joyful festivities. Mayor LaGuardia honored Randolph and the porters with a gala reception at New York's City Hall. LaGuardia used the occasion to praise Asa Randolph as "one of the foremost progressive labor leaders in America."

John L. Lewis, powerful leader of the Congress of Industrial Organizations, the CIO, gave Randolph full support. Born in Iowa in 1880, Lewis was a coal miner at age 12, and later became one of the most influential labor leaders in the United States. A friend to the Brotherhood, Lewis also became a powerful force in establishing labor reforms. Lewis advised Randolph to leave the AFL and join the CIO, reminding his friend that there would be less racial discrimination in the CIO. Randolph's response was firm. He preferred staying where he could fight the prejudice from within.

And he fought hard. During conventions and labor meetings, his elegantly attired figure became a familiar one on the platform. He preached for racial harmony as a necessary part of labor reforms. Most times, the suggestions Randolph proposed would be voted down. Undaunted, he would simply shrug his shoulders and walk with dignity to his seat. He had waited out the Pullman Company. One day, he believed, he would witness the end of racial discrimination in industry.

Success of the Brotherhood convinced Randolph that future civil rights reforms could be built upon a strong alliance between workers of varied racial and religious groups. He joined with a group of young, progressive African Americans that included E. Franklin Frazier, the noted historian; Ralph Bunche, who would later become the first African American to receive the Nobel Peace Prize (awarded in 1950 for his skillful settlement of the Israel-Arab conflict); and other scholarly activists. From this first meeting evolved the National Negro Congress (NNC). The group convinced Randolph that if he accepted its nomination for presidency, his popular and respected name would give credence to the organization.

Randolph accepted and promptly wrote an article to outline the major objectives of the NNC, stressing "the vital need of joint action and the tremendous value of working together." Randolph also helped to plan the first meeting, held in Chicago in February, 1936, with an interracial group of more than 800 persons in attendance, representing various types of organizations.

In his keynote address, Randolph challenged Roosevelt's plans for the economy saying, "The New Deal is no remedy. It does not seek to change the profit system. It does not place human rights above property rights, but gives the business interests the support of the state."

Delegates in attendance elected Randolph as president of the NNC and John P. Davis as the executive secretary, who would manage the organization on a daily basis.

At the second meeting held in Philadelphia in 1937, more than 1,100 attended with Walter White, the head of the NAACP, as one of the speakers. Hopes ran high for the NNC to become a leading organization to promote progress and race relations.

Many members voiced discontent, however, over the large attendance of Communists, a group Randolph had prevented from gaining influence in his Brotherhood. Their plan, he feared, was to take over the organization and control it for their own purposes. A crisis came during the 1940 convention held in Washington. By then, Randolph realized with certainty that Communists held the convention under their control, dominating committees and resolutions. When introduced as a speaker, Randolph boldly condemned the Communists for trying to wreck the congress. "American Negroes," he warned, "will not long follow orders from Moscow." Communists shouted to drown out Randolph's voice, then walked out of the convention hall while he was still speaking. Typical of Randolph, he stood tall and dignified, completing his speech as though nobody had left.

Later, however, he announced that he was leaving the National Negro Congress and stated his reasons, emphasizing that, "When the National Negro Congress loses its independence, it loses its soul and has no further reason for being. It also forfeits and betrays the faith of the Negro masses."

When Randolph left the NNC, other black members followed him. He still remained committed to obtaining justice and human rights for black Americans, for all Americans. By the 1940s, experience had taught him that the fight for justice and human rights could be waged in many ways and adapted to the time and the targets.

9
"THE TIME IS NOW!"
1935–1963

"There was no other group of Negroes in America who constituted the key to unlocking the door of a nationwide struggle for Negro rights as the porters. Without the porters, I couldn't have carried on the fight for fair employment, or the fight against discrimination in the armed forces."

—A. Philip Randolph

The formation of the Congress of Industrial Organization, the CIO, in 1935 brought revolutionary changes to the labor movement. The campaign of the new organization to bring black workers into this labor configuration proved that black and white workers brought together in unions could add strength and unity to the labor movement, and also eliminate the practice of bringing in black workers only as strike breakers.

The revolutionary change came largely because of constant, insistent appeals from Randolph and other far-thinking labor leaders who could foresee that prejudice would diminish with the building of strong interracial labor unions. Randolph insisted, in his testimony before the Senate and House Committees, that the Railway Act be amended in 1934 to include Pullman porters as well as other railway workers. This amendment gave the Brotherhood added strength and determination. In May, 1935, the porters proved by their votes that the Brotherhood would represent the black porters employed on the Pullman sleeping cars.

Prejudice and racism still persisted, but many of the CIO supporters helped in promoting the new labor laws to bring black workers into the union. The goals Randolph set were broader and more far-sighted. Black workers, he vowed, would eventually win equal roles in labor unions and in the United States government. In the 1940s, Randolph had used the threat of mass action to persuade President Roosevelt to initiate reforms that would lead to human rights for all American citizens. At mid-century Asa Randolph celebrated his sixty-first birthday, although he looked at least 10 years younger than his age. With the sudden death of Franklin Roosevelt in 1945, Vice President Harry S Truman assumed the office as President. Among his first official acts was the initiation of a draft bill mandating that eligible young men register for military service. America's army and navy were still segregated.

Bayard Rustin, who had helped to organize the Congress of Racial Equality (CORE) as well as the 1941 planned MOW (see chapter 1), was invited by Randolph to organize a new committee to protest against segregation in the military. Because of his opposition to wars and his refusal to be drafted, Rustin had been confined for nearly three years in a federal prison. Brilliant and talented, Rustin used his prison years to refine his skills—art, music and writing. In 1947, he again stood ready to use those skills in whatever role Randolph assigned him.

His skills were needed in the late 1940s. President Truman called for a peacetime draft which proposed universal military training. The 1947 draft bill did not, however, include a ban against segregation in the military. This, Randolph wrote in a press statement, was "pregnant with indecency."

By November, Randolph had joined with Grant Reynolds, the Commissioner of Corrections for New York State and organized a new group, the Committee Against Jim Crow in Military Service and Training, which in 1948 expanded into the League for Nonviolent Civil Disobedience Against Military Segregation. Bayard Rustin, then thirty-eight years old, agreed to serve as executive secretary, the position which would really run the League.

In March, 1948, at the invitation of President Truman, Randolph joined a group of black leaders for a visit in the White House. Also included in the conference were Walter White,

A. Philip Randolph (right) and Grant Reynolds (left) testifying. (UPI/ Bettmann)

Lester Granger of the National Urban League, Mary McLeod Bethune and Charles Houston, a special counsel for the NAACP.

The meeting proceeded in a friendly manner for a time until Randolph spoke directly and bluntly to Truman noting that the sentiment among Negroes of the country was that they would never bear arms again until all forms of bias and discrimination were abolished. Randolph continued, then made his main point, that those gathered were calling for an Executive Order abolishing segregation in the armed services. Truman repeatedly gave no direct answer, but thanked his guests for coming and ended the meeting.

President Truman's abrupt ending of the conference did not curtail Randolph at all. Nine days later, he appeared with Grant Reynolds and spoke before the Senate Armed Services Committee.

"This time Negroes will not take a Jim Crow draft lying down," Randolph told the group. "The conscience of the world will be shaken as by nothing else when thousands and thousands of us second-class Americans choose imprisonment in preference to permanent military slavery. . . . I personally will advise Negroes to refuse to fight as slaves for a democracy they cannot possess and cannot enjoy. . . . I personally pledge myself to openly counsel, and abet youth, both white and Negro, to guarantee any Jim Crow conscription system."

Senator Wayne Morse of Oregon interjected a question. "But you will expect . . . that there would not be any other course of action of our Government to follow but indictments for treason?"

"We would be willing to absorb the violence, absorb the terrorism, to face the music and to take whatever comes, and we, as a matter of fact, consider that we are more loyal to our country than the people who perpetrate segregation and discrimination upon Negroes because of color or race," replied Randolph.

President Dwight Eisenhower and A. Philip Randolph photographed with leaders following their conference on school integration and other matters affecting black citizens. (UPI/Bettmann)

Neither Wayne Morse nor any of the committee members could deter Randolph. Nor could many citizens of Harlem comprehend his boldness and courage. Congressman Adam Clayton Powell forwarded a statement to the Armed Services Committee, stating that Randolph's testimony "did most emphatically state the mood of the vast majority of the 15,000,000 colored Americans."

Randolph continued his consistent crusading for integrated armed services. At the Democratic National Convention in July, 1948, he could be seen with a picket sign that read: "PRISON IS BETTER THAN ARMY JIM CROW SERVICE."

The persistent pressure paid dividends. On July 26, 1948, President Truman issued Executive Order 9981, which stipulated a rapid end to military discrimination. When Randolph received assurance that the order would ban segregation in the military, he finally ended his campaign of civil disobedience. He also sent congratulations to President Truman, complimenting him for his statesmanship and courage.

By the 1950s, the civil rights movement had hit high gear. The "Journey of Reconciliation" had challenged the rigid segregation on interstate travel through states of the South. The 1954 *Brown* Supreme Court decision mandated racial integration of public schools. Following in rapid sequence, the Montgomery bus boycott, the formation of the Southern Christian Leadership Conference (SCLC), and the brave stand of the Little Rock Nine to integrate schools in Arkansas all combined to script a new chapter of the escalating movement for human rights.

The bravery of the Little Rock Nine had evoked admiration of supporters around the world. In the fall of 1957, the nine students volunteered to carry out the court-ordered integration of Central High School in Little Rock, Arkansas. Supporters again followed the drama as the students withstood irate howling mobs and insults from teachers, other students and parents. President Dwight D. Eisenhower finally announced on radio and television that he had "issued an Executive Order directing the use of troops." With troops keeping the crowds at bay, the nine bravely entered Central High.

Featured daily in newspapers and television, the courage of the nine had far-reaching impact upon the mounting determination to end legal racial segregation in the United States.

These students had dramatized the willingness of African Americans to face danger, even death, in order to end psychological slavery.

Throughout the ordeal, Mrs. Daisy Bates, president of the Arkansas chapter of the NAACP, knew that she placed her life and her home in danger. Yet, she continued to counsel the nine, exhibiting the determination and bravery that typified participants in the mushrooming revolution for human rights. The nine expressed the mood of the New Negro—determined, confident, fearless.

Other nations of the world were being reshaped by historic changes. In 1957, as one of several invited American dignitaries, including Martin and Coretta King, Randolph witnessed the historic change that took place in Ghana, West Africa. Minutes before midnight on March 5, the new flag of Ghana was raised to signal the nation's independence. In tribal languages, the natives shouted their joy: "Ghana is free!"

After the African American guests returned home, several of them met in New York to plan a freedom demonstration. The group included Roy Wilkins, elected NAACP president after Walter White died of a heart attack in 1955, Dr. King and Asa Randolph. From their discussions they developed strategies for a Prayer Pilgrimage to the nation's Capitol. Throughout the planning, Dr. King stressed that, "Our job is implementation. . . . We must move on to mass action."

The Prayer Pilgrimage set the stage. May 17, 1957, became "Pilgrimage Day." Thousands of pilgrims from 33 states formed a mass demonstration to pray for freedom at the steps of the Lincoln Memorial. On that day, listeners heard the voices of two of America's most eloquent speakers: Asa Philip Randolph and Dr. Martin Luther King, Jr. It was the voice of Randolph that electrified listeners when he announced: "I give you Martin Luther King!"

The mass demonstration brought an estimated fifty thousand citizens from across the country to pray and to protest the slow pace at which racial integration was taking place. Many listeners in the Prayer Pilgrimage March, as well as Americans at home, heard for the first time the voice of the young minister from Montgomery, Alabama. In his spellbinding speech, Dr. King emphasized the right to vote, still denied to most African Americans in states of the Deep

South. Television sets had become improved to enable viewers at home to join the marchers as they echoed the young minister's demand for voting rights. In a call-and-response pattern, the pilgrims repeated his phrasings.

"Give us the ballot! Give us the ballot! and we will no longer plead to the Federal government. . . ."

"Give us the ballot! Give us the ballot! and we will quietly and nonviolently, without rancor or bitterness implement the Supreme Court decision of May 17, 1954. . . ."

King's "Give us the ballot!" speech signalled acceleration of the modern civil rights movement. For Asa Randolph, the dream of a massive movement was shifted to the forefront of his thinking.

The issue of school integration remained high on Randolph's agenda, and it became the main topic for a conference on June 23, 1958, between President Dwight Eisenhower and a few civil rights leaders that included Asa Randolph, Martin Luther King, Jr., Roy Wilkins from the NAACP, and Lester Granger from the Urban League.

Completely confident with Presidents, Randolph presented Eisenhower with a program of action that included holding a White House Conference on school integration. The other leaders joined Randolph in urging Eisenhower to announce " a clear national policy and a program of implementation. . . ."

President Eisenhower voiced no objections to the plans for school integration. Still, he failed to take any major action to implement the mandate.

Randolph, a man of action, called together in 1958 an interracial meeting of one hundred citizens for a conference in New York. From this meeting grew the impetus for a Youth March for Integrated Schools, scheduled to take place in Washington, D.C., on October 11, 1958. During an outdoor rally in Harlem, Randolph explained the goal of the Youth March, saying, "The Children's March in Washington was conceived as a method of giving dramatization to the whole civil rights struggle." He also emphasized another aim: to arouse the conscience of America.

On the day following the Harlem rally, Martin Luther King was stabbed in the chest in a Harlem store while autographing his first book, *Stride Toward Freedom*. The attacker was later declared to be deranged and given medical treatment. King survived, but remained hospitalized until he was out of danger.

The Youth March took place on October 25. Numbering 9,500, the interracial marchers included students from fourth grade to college level who came to Washington in buses, cars and trains.

Under clear blue skies, the March extended down Constitution Avenue and on to the Lincoln Memorial. Adults leading the students included Asa Randolph; Harry Belafonte, the popular musician; Jackie Robinson, the star baseball player; and Coretta Scott King, taking the place of her husband, who was still recuperating from his stabbing.

From the steps of the Lincoln Memorial, the speakers, adults and students reminded the public of the nation's problems regarding school integration. A small delegation of students, led by Harry Belafonte, took a petition to the president requesting him to issue a statement declaring school integration "morally right as well as legally required." The students were not allowed to enter the White House grounds, nor could they speak with any of the president's secretaries.

Undaunted, Randolph helped to organize a second Youth March. This time, leaders of both races were invited to assist with the planning.

On April 18, 1959, 22,500 marchers listened to Dr. King, who had recovered. Other speakers included Roy Wilkins and Tom Mbaya, Chairman of the All Africa Peoples Conference.

President Eisenhower's deputy assistant met with Randolph, accompanied by an interracial group of students. The assistant relayed the president's best wishes along with a message that he would not be satisfied until all racial discrimination in the United States had disappeared. In response, Randolph and the students sent the president a petition asking for speedy action on the integration of public schools. Another group of students took a similar petition to members of Congress.

President Eisenhower sent a letter of thanks to the young people. He promised to take action that would lead to the end of racial discrimination.

Meanwhile, revolutionary changes continued in America and the world. In labor, the merger of the AFL and CIO forged a combined membership of approximately 15 million workers, with a large percentage of them African Americans. Randolph along with Willard Townsend, of the United Transport Service Employees, became the first black Americans to be appointed vice presidents, signaling the emerging strength of the black race in labor forces. Randolph used his position to encourage the AFL–CIO leaders to give greater support to civil rights reforms.

Racist attitudes toward black American workers gradually lessened. The powerful labor leaders, such as George Meany, demanded racial integration of union meetings, which took place in facilities with integrated policies and practices.

Meanwhile, American workers and citizens were being captivated by the determination and drama of the escalating revolution for civil rights, non-violent but militantly determined. The non-violent militancy that had been Randolph's trademark became a model that motivated young Americans and placed them suddenly as leaders of a revolution, designed to be peaceful, but made violent by those too transfixed to believe the truth: "Change must come!"

The emergence of clearer television screens brought the civil rights drama into homes. No citizen could hide from what was happening. The crusade for human rights became a daily lesson in courage, determination and belief in the American creed: "We hold these truths. . . ."

The scenes seared heart and conscience. Young students, white and black, left college and became freedom fighters, sensing that such a revolution might never come again, and that on the outcome rested the fate of the nation and their futures.

By the 1960s, Randolph was considered one of the most active and courageous citizens in the United States. He worked simultaneously on many fronts. In 1960, he helped to form the Negro American Labor Council (NALC), serving as president. The Council, he explained, would work to eliminate racism "in every area of the American labor movement." Through the NALC, Randolph worked to eliminate racial segregation from all labor unions. Another invaluable contribution of NALC was the motivation of members to take lead roles in the civil rights revolution that gathered momentum in the late 1950s, and suddenly exploded into action in the 1960s.

President John F. Kennedy with civil rights leaders. From left to right, front row: Whitney Young (National Urban League); Martin Luther King (Southern Christian Leadership Conference); Rabbi Joachim Prinz (Chairman of the American Jewish Council); A. Philip Randolph (Vice President of the AFL–CIO); President Kennedy; Walter Reuther (President of the United Auto Workers). (UPI/Bettmann)

The idea was translated into interracial planning sessions for a massive march on Washington. Rustin was given the green light to plan a new MOWM. Demonstrations for freedom must include the twin element of jobs, Randolph believed.

So it was that the 1963 March on Washington Movement became an updated and broadened plan of the MOWM that persuaded another president to support new civil rights reforms.

Randolph and Rustin planned with creative vision. Letters went out to heads of civil rights organizations inviting them to help bring at least 100,000 persons to the nation's capital for a March on Washington. The announcement motivated hundreds of citizens to begin planning. There were others who hesitated at first, fearful of what might happen during a huge interracial gathering.

One American with grave doubts was John Fitzgerald Kennedy, who in 1961 at age 43 became the youngest man ever elected to the presidency of the United States. A new civil rights bill he had sent to Congress requested sweeping reforms, and Kennedy worried that a demonstration in Washington might cause many Congressmen to veto the new bill.

In early June, President Kennedy called the march leaders to a conference. Randolph, having conferred personally with every American president since Calvin Coolidge, went with confidence.

Kennedy revealed he was opposed to the march. He cited the risk of violence in the streets which could harm the civil rights efforts. Randolph's answer was blunt. "Mr. President, the Negroes are already in the streets."

Dr. King added ideas that the planned march "could also serve as a means of dramatizing the issue and mobilizing support. . . ."

President Kennedy finally agreed to give support to the march. Privately, he still worried.

A. Phillip Randolph photographed in a pensive mood beside the Lincoln Memorial. (UPI/Bettmann)

Randolph quietly accepted the time-consuming duties despite a personal sadness during the busy months of planning the march. Lucille, his beloved "Buddy," had become bedridden from crippling arthritis. Randolph secured the help of nurses to be with her when he had to attend crucial meetings, but he assumed the duties of personal nurse much of the time. He carefully prepared Lucille's favorite foods the way she liked them. When she could not feed herself, he fed her. Every evening he sat beside the bed and read aloud to her, his deep voice filling the room until she fell asleep.

Meanwhile, in his quiet, efficient manner, Bayard Rustin masterminded the logistics of the March. He would later recall the innumerable details he handled, the countless questions he had to answer. "What should people bring in a lunch box on a hot day in August?" "What about facilities?" To answer such questions, Rustin sent out printed booklets, detailing every personal problem a marcher might face regarding comfort or safety.

August 28 dawned in Washington, D.C., with clear skies. During the early morning, Randolph and other leaders conferred with key members of Congress. Meanwhile, thousands streamed into Washington by the hour. For one glorious day, the barriers of race or religion or economic status seemed totally irrelevant. Americans laughed and sang and ate together under the tent of a unifying universe. Many hoisted signs with the focus printed: "JOBS AND FREEDOM!" They enjoyed the thoughtful activities Rustin and his team had carefully planned to keep the marchers comfortable, happy, entertained and motivated.

Randolph, age 74, walked in the front line of dignitaries, leading the throng toward the Lincoln Memorial. His long dream of a MOWM was finally realized. An estimated 250,000 marchers walked behind the line of distinguished notables. They represented a cross-section of America's racial, religious, ethnic and economic backgrounds.

"Let the nation and the world know the meaning of our numbers!" Randolph's rich voice boomed the words through the microphones. "We are an advanced guard of a massive revolution for jobs and freedom."

The long program of speeches and music kept the crowd waiting in anticipation. Then Randolph called out the name that brought thundering waves of applause.

Dr. Martin Luther King, Jr., stepped to the speaker's podium and the applause acknowledged him as the foremost African-American leader of the era. Listening to his beautifully prepared speech, the crowd applauded. When he shifted to his more personal style as a son and grandson of Baptist ministers, the crowd became electrified—cheering, weeping, answering, praying. Each time King intoned phrases such as "Let freedom ring," many in the crowd echoed the words, "Let freedom ring!" By the time he came to, "Free at last," marchers were weeping and embracing one another, friends and strangers alike.

Bayard Rustin read the Demands of the March, outlining a program to end job discrimination. In closing, Randolph read the March Pledge, citing a commitment to fight for social justice.

"I do so pledge!" the throng responded.

The day Randolph described as "most beautiful and glorious" came to a close. As the thousands of marchers slowly dispersed in later afternoon, Bayard Rustin found him standing alone, with tears streaming down his cheeks. Rustin stood in understanding silence beside his mentor, knowing that the tears probably flowed because his beloved Buddy had not lived to share the glorious day. Lucille had died three months earlier.

Randolph's tears may also have flowed in happiness for the sheer magnificence of the March and the vision it evoked of racial and religious harmony. The day had, indeed, brought a vision of an America "most beautiful and glorious."

The Freedom Movement escalated. New and younger African Americans criticized the slow-paced leadership styles of older persons, even of Randolph and King. Brilliant, dedicated, impatient, many new leaders delayed their college training. "Freedom Now!" echoed across America, spoken and cheered by different voices from marchers with varying skin colors. The word "freedom" finally evoked among countless Americans the dream of "freedom and justice" for all.

Asa Philip Randolph had reached the realization that goals and tactics must be altered with changing times. Fast, high-powered jet airplanes rapidly eliminated the need for Pullman porters and parlor cars. In September, 1968, Randolph retired from his position as president of his beloved Brotherhood. His sights were set toward encompassing goals that could include all workers, all genders, all races of the world.

10

ENDURING LEGACY
1964–1979

> "The question is not whether we have the means. The question is whether we have the will. Ten years from now, will two-fifths of our nation still live in poverty and deprivation? This is, above all, a moral question. And upon the answer hangs not only the fate of the Negro—weighed down by centuries of exploitation, degradation, and malice—but the fate of the nation."
>
> —A. Philip Randolph

Throughout Asa Randolph's years of writing, speaking and forming alliances, he never sought the financial gains he could have garnered. His lifestyle remained modest and unpretentious as he continued crusading for human rights, working for the masses of poor people.

As the Freedom Movement escalated in the 1960s, new leaders and revolutionary tactics reshaped its goals and pacing. Younger black Americans, many of them leaving college to join the revolutionary crusading, had no patience for the slow, methodical planning and pleading of the past. With the call for "freedom now," they swept away walls that had separated racial groups and held descendants of slaves in a prison known as "segregation." Amazing to the world, descendants of slave-holders joined the descendants of slaves in marches and sit-ins. Freedom riders ushered in a revised and revolutionary era that eliminated walls of separation as though they were mere hindrances to a new world of oneness and caring.

A. Philip Randolph and Martin Luther King, Jr., in a discussion before the opening of the White House Conference on Civil Rights, with a call for a $100 billion "Freedom Budget" to wipe out black ghettos in U.S. cities. (UPI/Bettmann)

Active on many fronts, Randolph worked, revolutionizing customs and laws that had excluded the black race and the poor from human rights that legally were the inheritance of all citizens. The passage of new laws enabled descendants of slaves to realize the power of their collective strength as they listened to men such as Randolph and Dr. King, generally considered two of the top leaders of America.

The March on Washington helped to broaden the base of the civil rights movement, and more and more people, young and old, rich and poor, black and white, became part of it. Randolph and other thoughtful citizens realized, however, that the thrust for jobs and freedom was only at a beginning stage, and that countless problems remained to be solved. To be successful, civil rights efforts needed supportive actions in order for citizens to gain economic rights.

Acting on this thesis, Randolph initiated another project to benefit workers, especially those who were black and often poor. In 1964, with a generous grant from the AFL-CIO and other wealthy friends, the A. Philip Randolph Institute was established in Harlem with plans for a network of affiliates in various sections of the United States. A primary focus of the Institute included recruitment of young black youth and training them in the skills required for working, especially in the construction trades, and to help them overcome hardships and problems that might prevent their moving to high-salaried positions. The varied programs for the institute included ideas from experts in labor and industry. The Randolph Institute also planned "to insure the power of the poor through voter education and registration."

With continued reminders from Randolph and other activists, black workers became increasingly more vocal on issues of civil rights and challenged unfair practices and laws. The Randolph Institute later gave assistance to the sanitation workers of Memphis, Tennessee, and to the grape pickers of California during their strikes. Both groups eventually won an important right they sought, the right to bargain collectively.

In explaining the Freedom Budget, Randolph insisted that, "In this, the richest and most productive society ever known to man, the scourge of poverty can and must be abolished . . . within the next 10 years!" With help from economists, a budget was drawn up recommending an expenditure of $18.5 billion

annually over a 10-year period. The proposal sought to eliminate the major causes of poverty in the United States. Built
into Randolph's theory was the plan that the assistance
received would not be in the form of welfare but as an
assured income which would be used to purchase goods and
services. The plan, Randolph explained, would assure that
citizens have the financial ability to purchase goods and
services, leading to the need for further production and,
therefore, for jobs. Such a plan, Randolph explained, would
lead to a more stable economy. It would also mandate a
reordering of the nation's priorities.

Randolph's Freedom Budget was never adopted or ade-
quately funded by the federal government and, therefore,
never had the impact envisioned by the planners. Disappointed, but philosophical, he moved on to other problems.

Under the masterful guidance of Bayard Rustin as director
and Cleveland Robinson, a co-organizer of the March on Washington, as his assistant, the Institute expanded. Believing that
civil rights alone could not assure needed changes, Randolph
set dual goals for the institute: civil rights and economic
equality. This combination, he believed, could eliminate most
of the evil and unrest that plagued the world.

A problem in Montgomery, Alabama, suddenly shifted Randolph's attention. Martin Luther King was arrested in his
office by two local deputies on charges of perjury, a felony, for
falsely documenting his 1956 and 1958 income tax. This accu-
sation, if proven true, could ruin his reputation and, worse,
harm the Freedom Movement.

With Randolph as chairman, a group of New York friends
formed the "Committee to Defend Martin Luther King" and
mounted a fund-raising goal of $200,000 for King's legal de-
fense and also for a voter registration plan. Randolph agreed
to be chairman, with Rustin as executive director. With a team
of astute lawyers to defend him, King was found not guilty and
the morning after his acquittal, the topic of the sermon he
preached in Ebenezer Church was titled "Autobiography of
Suffering."

As the Movement for Social Change expanded, Randolph
continued his close alliance with King. During the crucial
period, he had encouraged Rustin to visit Montgomery and use
his organizational genius to help plan ways of transporting

workers to and from their jobs during the continued bus boycott. Rustin's admiration for King's leadership had motivated him to team with Ella Baker in 1958 and plan the establishment of the Southern Christian Leadership Conference (SCLC), an organization of citizens united to fight race prejudice and, as Rustin advised, to also "maintain the psychological momentum Montgomery has generated."

Throughout the 1960s, the call for "Freedom Now" reverberated in states of the Deep South despite acts of violence, calculated to frighten anyone who dared to question racist rules and actions. Any mention of change invited punishment by racists who knew they would probably never be brought to trial. In 1967, Medgar Evers, a NAACP official, was shot to death in the driveway of his home in Jackson, Mississippi.

Nevertheless, a project called Freedom Summer brought hundreds of white student volunteers to travel to Mississippi to begin a huge voter registration drive. The project would show that blacks and whites could work together in harmony. Of the 800 students who volunteered, 300 were chosen.

The day after the students arrived, three young men—Andrew Goodman, James Chaney and Michael Schwerner disappeared and their bodies were later found shot to death and buried on a farm. All 21 of the white men tried for the murders were released, but later a federal court tried the case and seven of them were sent to jail.

Some of the white students left, but the majority stayed, even though the violence against blacks continued. Barred from the Mississippi Democratic Party, black citizens, with the help of Ella Baker, organized the Mississippi Freedom Democratic Party, the MFDP.

Meanwhile, an interracial group of young students decided to help black citizens of the Deep South in their crusade for voting rights. The Student Nonviolent Coordinating Committee (SNCC) chose Alabama and Mississippi, known for their hardcore segregation practices. Captained by Robert Moses, the field secretary of SNCC, the thrust in Mississippi was the Freedom Summer Project, organized to help black citizens obtain the right to vote.

During the 1964 Democratic National Convention held in Atlantic City, New Jersey, the regular Democratic party for Mississippi

Fannie Lou Hamer of the Mississippi Freedom Democratic Party who, in one of the dramatic moments of the Democratic National Convention, walks firmly toward the entrance to the convention hall, to which she and other members of her group were finally admitted. (UPI/Bettmann)

Mrs. Coretta Scott King, widow of Dr. Martin Luther King, Jr., congratulates A. Philip Randolph at a birthday in his honor.   (UPI/Bettmann)

had only white delegates. The MFDP, an interracial group, was refused seating, nevertheless, Fannie Lou Hamer, who had been fired from her job and beaten by police for attempting to register, seized the microphone and delivered a speech to the convention which was carried to the nation by television later that evening, giving her and the project immediate fame. These brave actions resulted in changes. The National Democratic Party ruled that state delegations would be racially mixed in the future elections. Voting rights expanded in the South.

Many of the changes came as a result of unselfish actions of citizens such as Asa Philip Randolph. On April 15, 1969, his 80th birthday was celebrated at a gala gathering of 1,300 people at the Waldorf Astoria Hotel in New York City. Attendants represented the variety of personalities, projects, causes and movements Randolph had helped to initiate or promote. The many speakers who lauded his accomplishments included Coretta Scott King, New York's governor Nelson Rockefeller and many other notable personalities. April 15, Randolph's birthday, was declared "A. Philip Randolph Day" throughout the state of New York.

When the quiet, unassuming, but always elegant guest of honor stood to speak, the gathering gave him an applause befitting the Chief. Randolph viewed the celebration as a "rededication to a cause to which I have contributed my energies, and to principles to which I have dedicated my life. The cause has been the liberation of the Negro in America."

Randolph's closing statement challenged the guests assembled.

> "We must draw upon the capacity of human beings to act with humanity towards one another. We must draw upon the human potential for kindness and decency. And we must have faith that this society, divided by race and by class, and subject to profound social pressures, can one day become a nation of equals, and banish white racism and black racism and anti-Semitism to the limbs of oblivion from which they shall never emerge."

On May 16, 1979, A. Philip Randolph died at age 90. His unselfish, insistent demand for justice and freedom remains an enduring legacy to all Americans and to the world. His life and legacy remain a constant inspiration to the generations for which he crusaded and all that follow.

The Freedom Budget was never funded to the extent that the goals could be met and measured. Realizing that he was often years ahead of the thinking of many other leaders, Randolph could take pride in the many changes he had witnessed and been a part of in nearly a century of crusading.

Honored as one of the most outstanding black citizens of his nation, he never tried to use the movements or causes he championed to raise his popularity level, never to gain riches.

He never owned a house or a car, items most people deem essential. His movements, speeches and crusades were always for the betterment of the country he loved, and the people he served. Asa Philip Randolph's legacy will last for generations to come.

SOURCES AND SELECTED
BIBLIOGRAPHIES

Sources

The *Asa Philip Randolph Papers* in the Manuscript Division of the Library of Congress are testament to the diversity of citizens and leaders with whom he corresponded in America and in other sections of the world.

The Chicago Historical Society, as well as the Schomburg Collection of the New York Public Library, are among other archives that preserve a treasury of information on Randolph's varied accomplishments.

Conditions during his early life in Jacksonville, Florida, can be realized from James Weldon Johnson's autobiography, *Along This Way*.

The *Messenger*, now available in bound volumes in many libraries, including those of colleges and universities, gives examples of Randolph's interests and accomplishments and his fearlessness in protesting injustice wherever it occurred. Articles and photographs in the *Messenger* show the changing styles of clothing from year to year, the rising recognition of women in American life, and the increase in economic levels of black citizens, illustrated by homes, positions, accomplishments, statements, etc.

The migration of other black citizens from the southern states of America, as well as from the West Indies, is told and illustrated by many excellent writers, including James Weldon Johnson's *Black Manhattan* (New York, Atheneum, 1930, 1968), and Gilbert Osofsky in *Harlem: The Making of a Ghetto* (New York: Harper, 1968). These and other interesting publications illustrate the making of Harlem into a ghetto as more black Americans and West Indians were forced to crowd into dwellings left by white families who ran to escape from mingling with waves of black newcomers.

The historical background of the Brotherhood of Sleeping Car Porters and their struggle to become organized can be traced through issues of the *Messenger*.

Details of the March on Washington Movement in the 1940s can be found in *When Negroes March* by Herbert Garfinkel (Atheneum, 1969), *In Confrontation Black and White* by Lerone Bennett (Penguin, 1966), *Eleanor and Franklin* by Joseph P. Lash (Norton, 1971), and in *A Man Called White*, the autobiography of Walter White (University of Georgia Press, 1995).

An excellent account of Asa Randolph's "Freedom Budget For All Americans" is given in *Mr. Black Labor* by Daniel S. Davis (E. P. Dutton, 1922).

The significance of Asa Randolph's work in organizing and motivating the porters includes the fact that many of them became leaders in their communities and leaders in the crusade for civil rights. Randolph's role in assisting Martin Luther King, Jr., with his movement for equality and justice illustrates his unselfishness in working for the benefit of others, with little action to seek notoriety for himself.

Additional Sources

Several sources present information on the development of the Pullman Parlor Cars and the important role members of the Brotherhood of Pullman Porters played in the expansion of America. These include Bradford R. Brazeal's *The Brotherhood of Sleeping Car Porters: Its Origin and Development* (New York, Harper and Brothers, 1946), which presents a study of the Brotherhood and their accomplishments from the early days of Pullman cars.

Another story of the porters from the early days of Pullman cars is *A Long Hard Journey* by Patricia and Frederick McKissack (Walker & Company, 1990). Through interesting, easy-to-read text and numerous photographs, the development of the Pullman Sleeping Cars and the contribution of the porters who helped to make them popular becomes a fascinating part of America's history.

Miles of Smiles, Years of Struggle: Stories of Black Pullman Porters (University of Chicago Press, 1989) includes numerous anecdotes gleaned from personal accounts of Pullman porters who occupied a position classified by many of them as the "highest status in the black community and the lowest on the train."

Philip S. Foner's *Organized Labor and the Black Worker, 1619–1973* (New York: Praeger Publishers, 1974) includes numerous references to Randolph and underscores the significance of the roles he played in raising the position of black workers in America's labor arena.

Another rich source on Randolph and the Pullman porters is William H. Harris's *Keeping the Faith: A. Philip Randolph, Milton P. Webster, and the Brotherhood of Sleeping Car Porters, 1925–1937* (Urbana, University of Illinois Press, 1977). The story of the long struggle waged by the Brotherhood of Porters with the Pullman Company to have their union and the pivotal role of Asa Randolph and the porters to "keep the faith" illustrate the unselfish determination of the porters and their leaders.

Benjamin Quarles's *A. Philip Randolph: Labor Leader at Large* in *Black Leaders of the Twentieth Century* (University of Illinois Press, 1986) presents a serious and superb analysis of Randolph's role as a black leader and his accomplishment, presented by a noted scholar and historian.

Books that present Asa Randolph's story for young readers include: *A. Philip Randolph* by Sally Hanley (Chelsea House Publishers, 1989). Hanley presents essential facts and accomplishments of Randolph's life in an easy-to-understand style.

Equally easy to understand is *A. Philip Randolph: Integration in the Workplace* by Sarah Wright (Silver Burdett Press, Inc., 1990). In seventeen brief chapters with numerous photographs, the author presents a perceptive portrait of Asa Randolph, and of the years during which he unselfishly crusaded to assure equal rights for workers and for all citizens in every aspect of American life.

Bulletins, pamphlets, and periodical literature published by Randolph served as motivating and instructional materials for all readers, particularly those in black communities and those who were workers. *The Black Worker*, a newsletter published with a grant from the Garland Fund, was printed primarily to instruct, inform, and communicate with workers, especially the Pullman porters.

For Additional Reading

Bontemps, Arna. *One Hundred Years of Negro Freedom*. New York: Dodd Mead & Co., 1961.

Dallard, Shyler. *Ella Baker*. New York: Silver Burdett Press, 1990.

Kornweibel, Theodore, Jr. *No Crystal Stair: Black Life and the Messenger, 1919–1928*. Greenwood Publishing Group, Inc., 1975.

Lash, Joseph. *Eleanor and Franklin*. New York: W. W. Norton & Co., 1971.

Osofsky, Gilbert. *Harlem: The Making of a Ghetto, 1890–1930*. New York: Harper Collins Publishers, 1971.

Schuyler, George S. *Black and Conservative: The Autobiography of George S. Schuyler*. Nashville: Abingdon Press, 1966.

White, Walter. *A Man Called White: The Autobiography of Walter White*. Athens: University of Georgia Press, 1995.

Woodward, C. Vann. Editor. *Down the Line: The Collected Writings of Bayard Rustin*. New York: Anti-Defamation League of B'nai B'rith, 1985.

INDEX

Italic page numbers indicate illustrations.

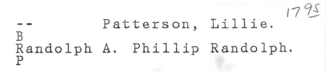

--   Patterson, Lillie.   1795
B
Randolph A. Phillip Randolph.
P

DATE			